D1265029

PATHWAYS TO CERTAINTY

PATHWAYS
TO CERTAINTY

BY

WILLIAM ADAMS BROWN, Ph.D., D.D.

CHARLES SCRIBNER'S SONS
NEW YORK · LONDON
1930

TO

HELEN

DAUGHTER

WELL BELOVED

"O world, thou choosest not the better part!
 It is not wisdom to be only wise,
 And on the inward vision close the eyes,
 But it is wisdom to believe the heart.
 Columbus found a world, and had no chart,
 Save one that faith deciphered in the skies;
 To trust the soul's invincible surmise
 Was all his science and his only art.
 Our knowledge is a torch of smoky pine
 That lights the pathway but one step ahead
 Across a void of mystery and dread.
 Bid, then, the tender light of faith to shine
 By which alone the mortal heart is led
 Unto the thinking of the thought divine."

—FROM "POEMS," BY GEORGE SANTAYANA.

PREFATORY NOTE

I wish to express my thanks to the many friends whose counsel has helped me to clarify my own thinking on this subject, on which, of all subjects, clear thinking is most essential. I am especially indebted to the members of the different groups, varying in number from fifty to several hundred, with whom from time to time, in Cleveland, in Hartford, in New York, in Halifax, and again in New York, it has been my privilege to think through the line of thought which is here presented in more systematic form.

To my colleagues, Professor Henry Pitney Van Dusen and Professor John Coleman Bennett, who have read the book in MS., I owe many helpful suggestions. My friend and former assistant, Professor Walter M. Horton, of Oberlin, has also been good enough to read the book in MS.

Of the help that has come to me through books, I have made acknowledgment at the appropriate place in the text. I wish especially to express my appreciation of a volume by Professor William P. Montague, of Columbia University, entitled *The Ways of Knowing*. In this book the author points out the different ways in which as a matter of fact we acquire knowledge and relates each to the particular philosophical theory with which it is most closely associated. The line of thought in the present work, while worked out independently, parallels at more than one point Professor Montague's suggestive reasoning.

Since beginning my book I have had the privilege of studying Professor John Dewey's Gifford Lectures on *The Quest for Certainty*, which deal with the same subject from a different angle. While recognizing much that is helpful and true in Professor Dewey's analysis of the contribution of reflective thought to the validation of our beliefs, and paying tribute to the moral earnestness which has led him to question the validity of convictions in which other thinkers have found serenity and solace, I believe that in his desire to guard against the dangers of uncontrolled speculation he has been led to underestimate the extent of the knowledge possible to us in the field of religion. I have, therefore, felt free to make a larger, although I trust not an uncritical, use of the more direct ways of approach to the apprehension of reality through which religious men in all ages have won their certainty of God.

It has been my aim, in the present study, so far as possible, to avoid all merely technical questions and to address myself to the problem of certainty in the simple and direct form in which it meets the men and women of our day who, in the conflicts of contemporary thought, are trying to find some firm foundation for a faith in themselves, in the world, and in God.

WILLIAM ADAMS BROWN.

UNION THEOLOGICAL SEMINARY, 1930.

I wish to thank Professor George Santayana for permission to quote the sonnet on page viii. Professor A. S. Eddington, Professor Sir James Jeans and Mr. Walter Lippmann have also kindly granted me permission to use quotations from their books. To the publishers of Baron von Hügel's Selected Letters, I am under obligation for the privilege of using an extensive quotation from a letter of the Baron to George Tyrrell.

CONTENTS

CONTENTS

CHAPTER V. THE WAY OF REASONING: OR THE TEST
OF CONSISTENCY

CHAPTER VI. THE WAY OF EXPERIMENT: OR THE PRAC-
TICE OF THE PRESENCE OF GOD

CHAPTER VII. THE CERTAINTY OF TO-DAY AND THE
HOPE FOR TO-MORROW

PATHWAYS TO CERTAINTY

Can we be certain of God? There are many people who tell us that we cannot. Some of them are glad of the fact and assure us that the thrill that comes to those who must bravely face the universe alone more than compensates for the loss of the satisfaction which men used to take in the divine companionship. Others are sorry and in their loneliness and isolation would gladly welcome any help toward a firm basis on which to build their lives. A common assumption underlies both attitudes, the assumption that something has happened that makes it no longer possible for a modern man to be sure of God.

This assumption we propose to examine. We shall try to show that those who make it fail adequately to distinguish between two types of certainty, the type which takes account only of such knowledge as may be attained through the exact sciences and which is reached by eliminating the qualitative elements in human life, and the type which makes room also for the values which life reveals and for the meanings which it suggests. Religion is concerned with certainty in the second sense. We hope to show that nothing which has been revealed by the researches of exact science renders the second type of certainty unattainable, although our modern way of expressing and clarifying it may differ considerably from the ways used in the past.

INTRODUCTION

WHY A NEW BOOK ON RELIGIOUS CERTAINTY

INTRODUCTION

WHY A NEW BOOK ON RELIGIOUS CERTAINTY

This is a book about certainty in religion. It has to do with those singular personal possessions which we call religious convictions, especially with the central conviction which expresses man's faith in the existence of a real God with whom he can have practical relations of worship and service. We shall ask whence this conviction comes and what it can do for us. Is it a tenable conviction, worthy of the acceptance of reasonable men, or is it, as some of our contemporaries would persuade us, simply an illusion, a garment woven out of our desires, with which we try to shield ourselves against the chill of the unknown? If it is a reasonable conviction, how happens it that so many in our day seem to have lost it? What can we do—indeed can we do anything—to win it back?

These questions have been the theme of philosophy in every age. For centuries the finest intellects of the race have grappled with them. What more, it may reasonably be asked, can be said about them which has not been said again and again?

But it is one thing to discuss religion as an academic question, quite another to achieve personal certainty on the issues at stake. One does not become sure of God simply by weighing the arguments which may be given for and against believing in him. A conviction is more than an opinion or a conjecture, more even than a belief. A conviction is a belief which has been personally appropriated and which has become a determining factor in life. To acquire religious conviction the assent of the mind is not enough. The whole personality must make its contribution, the emotions and the will as well as the intellect.

Students of psychology have recently been devoting attention to the problem of the genesis of conviction and they have much that is interesting and instructive to tell us. They have uncovered many hitherto unrecognized factors which enter into the making of our beliefs. Some of these factors are purely physical, such as the external environment in which we live, or the condition of our brain and nervous system; others are found in that mysterious part of ourselves that we call the subconscious, such as our impulses, our sentiments, and our dispositions. Psychology is charting for us this hitherto unfathomed sea and the charts are proving useful in helping us to steer our way past hidden reefs on which we might otherwise have suffered shipwreck. Of all these data we must take account.

But although we need to know all that psychology can teach us about the genesis of religious conviction we must be on our guard against an undiscriminating use of the psychologist's methods. Psychology is a new science and it is sometimes difficult to distinguish between its assured results and its untested theories. In the older sciences the testing of theory has gone so far that there is a body of accepted knowledge on which we can rely. In psychology, as the best psychologists recognize, the body of available knowledge is both smaller in amount and less trustworthy in character. But the anticipations of the learner often outrun the achievements of the teacher and in the popular press and on the platform all sorts of extravagant claims are being made for psychology, as though it already possessed the key to all that is necessary for human welfare and happiness. Dazzled by such promises, many of our contemporaries find the well-trodden paths that have been followed by earlier generations hopelessly antiquated. They no longer have faith in the older ways of winning certainty of God.

Under these conditions it has seemed to me that there was room for a study of religious certainty which, while heartily welcoming the new knowledge which psychology brings and making use of its methods so far as they prove helpful, should relate these methods to the older ways of approach to God. If the book brings to some readers little that is new, it may at least justify its existence by furnishing them with certain guideposts by which they can find their way more conveniently to the most helpful material already available.

For certainty in religion, we must never forget, unlike the certainty of science, where the expert has the right of way, must be won by each one of us for himself. The most that one man can do for another is to point the way and to suggest the steps that may lead to the desired goal. Whether the steps will be taken or not will depend in each case upon an act of individual choice. Even the most convinced authoritarian must still decide in what authority he will put his trust; and Church, and Bible, and Christ, and God himself, become ours only as we make them ours by that free assent which is the supreme expression of personality.

CHAPTER I

WHY WE NEED CERTAINTY IN RELIGION

A noticeable feature of contemporary religious life is the loss of the sense of certainty. One important reason for this loss is the widespread conviction that the only kind of certainty worth having is that which is reached by the methods of exact science. Science reaches its certainty by eliminating the qualitative element from its hypotheses and concentrating attention upon matters which are capable of quantitative test, a method which is manifestly inapplicable in the field of religion.

Yet the reasons which lead people to desire religious certainty were never stronger than to-day and the uses that it would serve, could it be had, were never more apparent.

The possibility of justifying the religious attitude in the face of the contemporary challenge depends upon our ability to show that the kind of certainty reached through the method of the exact sciences is not the only kind of certainty, but that in the qualitative field as well trustworthy knowledge is attainable. Non-theistic humanists admit the possibility of such knowledge within the limits set by our human relations, but deny the legitimacy of its extension to the cosmic friend whom religion calls God. To answer the humanist contention, therefore, we must show that this restriction is both unnecessary and unreasonable.

1. THE LOSS OF CERTAINTY IN CONTEMPORARY RELIGION

The Prevailing Uncertainty in Matters of Religion

In his suggestive book, *A Preface to Morals*,[1] Mr. Walter Lippmann calls attention to a striking feature of contemporary religion—its loss of the sense of certainty. Whatever one might think of the old religion, this at least could be said of it, that it was clearcut and positive. It presented men with definite doctrines to be believed, specific rules to be followed, and a supreme authority to which one could respond with unquestioning loyalty.

But to-day for many men the old unquestioning confidence is gone. They no longer believe what the old creeds say, yet they have not outgrown the needs of which the old creeds were the expression.

Mr. Lippmann has described with rare insight the plight in which many a modern man finds himself:

"There is no theory of the meaning and value of events which he is compelled to accept, but he is none the less compelled to accept the events. There is no moral authority to which he must turn now, but there is coercion in opinions, fashions and fads. There is for him no inevitable purpose in the universe, but there are elaborate necessities, physical, political, economic. He does not feel himself to be an actor in a great and dramatic destiny, but he is subject to the

[1] New York, 1929. By permission of the Macmillan Company, publishers.

9

massive powers of our civilization, forced to adopt their pace, bound to their routine, entangled in their conflicts. He can believe what he chooses about this civilization. He cannot, however, escape the compulsion of modern events. They compel his body and his senses as ruthlessly as ever did king or priest. They do not compel his mind. They have all the force of natural events, but not their majesty, all the tyrannical power of ancient institutions, but none of their moral certainty. Events are there, and they overpower him. But they do not convince him that they have that dignity which inheres in that which is necessary and in the nature of things.[2]

This change is the more noteworthy because it coincides with a great increase in our knowledge about religion. There has been no time since religion began when we knew as much about its origin, its history, and its present manifestations. For generations scholars have been bringing to its study the industry, the patience, and the open-mindedness which have won such signal triumphs in the field of the physical universe and the record of what they have discovered fills many libraries. If we are not certain about the truth of our religion, it is not for lack of knowledge in the sense in which science uses that term.

Explanation of This Uncertainty in a Narrow Conception of Certainty

But there is more than one kind of certainty and more than one way of reaching it. There is the certainty attained by science, in the conventional sense

[2] Pp. 9, 10.

of the term, and the certainty of common life. The certainty of science is reached by means of laboratory experiment from which all disturbing factors have been systematically eliminated and the result of which commands the assent of all competent observers. The certainty of common life involves personal factors which vary in the case of different individuals and which lead to correspondingly different conclusions.

In our daily living we seek certainty in both these senses and we find both indispensable. There is a side of our life in which we are dependent upon what science can tell us and we use its results with unquestioning confidence. Science sets our watches, constructs our calendars, builds our bridges, and runs our trains, and its ceaseless researches are constantly enlarging the area which it can not only explain but control.

But there is another side of our life which science is not as yet able to chart, but where certainty is even more important for us,—the world of our hopes and of our fears, of our aspirations and of our loyalties. There are persons to be loved and promises to be trusted, causes which command loyalty and faiths to be embraced. And here too we often find it possible to gain an assurance which is adequate for our personal need.

Even in the restricted field with which the exact sciences are more particularly concerned it is often necessary to distinguish between different kinds of certainty.

Some years ago the child of a neighbor was attacked by a malignant dysentery which was steadily sapping her strength and against which the best efforts of the physician in charge proved unavailing. At that time one of the great Foundations was experimenting with a serum for dysentery which had not yet been sufficiently tested to be made available to the profession. Through the courtesy of the physician in charge of the experiment a supply of the serum was obtained and it was administered to the patient with extraordinarily beneficial results. Almost immediately a change for the better took place and in a few days the child was pronounced out of danger.

A few days later I met an eminent specialist, who had been present when the serum was administered. "I suppose," I said to him, "that there can be no doubt that the serum saved the child's life." "If you ask me as a scientist," he replied, "I should have to say that thousands of additional experiments would need to be made before I should feel justified in expressing an opinion, but if you ask me as a human being, I have not the least doubt that the serum saved the child's life."

This answer well illustrates the contrast between the two kinds of certainty referred to: the certainty of science, in which so far as possible all subjective elements have been eliminated, and the certainty of common life, into which the factor of personal faith necessarily enters.

This distinction will help us to understand what

has been happening in the realm of religion. In the past the certainty which religion was supposed to guarantee has been frequently conceived after the analogy of the certainties of science. As science owes its authority to a source outside itself, namely the laws of nature which it discovers and does not invent, so religion traced its authority to a source no less independent—supernatural revelation, once for all given—and hence for all rational beings authoritative and final. And as the scientist can be satisfied with no proof which is not equally convincing to every one who is willing to examine the evidence, so the religious teacher professed to furnish man with an authority whose trustworthiness it was not possible for any open-minded man to doubt. Thus religion, like science, made complete objectivity its goal. For both, the certainty that was sought was independent of the fluctuations of individual opinion and hence equally valid for every one.

For many of our contemporaries this way of thinking of religious certainty presents all but insuperable difficulties. In making us better acquainted with the history of religion science has brought forcibly to our attention the subjective factors which enter into its making. Belief in a revelation that should mean the same thing for all men at all times is becoming increasingly difficult, and with its departure is going the unquestioning certainty which that belief brought to the men of an earlier generation. The conclusion is a natural one, that, since the kind of certainty which religious men have claimed for religion in the past is no longer attainable, all certainty that is worth while is at an end so far as the objects of religious faith are concerned.

This is in fact the conclusion to which Mr. Lippmann comes in the book already referred to. He dismisses as negligible all attempts to gain certainty in religion which do not yield results as definite as those of the traditional theology and bids us look for the practical certainty we need for the regulation of our daily life to other sources than religion.

In taking this position Mr. Lippmann is simply expressing with more than usual clarity and persuasiveness an attitude which is shared by many of his contemporaries. Having lost the certainty which the old religion gave them they are turning in other directions for substitutes to take its place. Some find the substitute of which they are in search in individual self-development, as it is made possible through the pursuit of science or the cultivation of the arts; others in the advancement of the social welfare in some one of its many forms. But they are all alike in this, that they have lost the consciousness of God which gave unity and security to the old religion. The object of their highest devotion is man, as he is or as he may become. If they are to have religion at all, it must be a humanist religion.

Illustrations in Contemporary Humanism

In speaking of humanism it is first of all necessary to define it. For the word is used to-day in two different and largely exclusive senses. As used by one group of contemporary writers,[2] it means a spiritual view of life, as opposed to a mechanistic view, and among those who accept or defend the humanist position are theists like Professor Paul Elmer More who stand in the classic Christian tradition.[3] But the word is also widely used to designate a way of looking at human life which tries to conserve the essential human values without the aid which is furnished by belief in God. It is humanism in this second, non-theistic, sense that we shall have primarily in mind in what follows.

This use of the name has been given currency by a group of radical American Unitarians who employ it to distinguish themselves from the more conservative members of the Unitarian body, who still hold the theistic faith.[4] But the word is also used to describe a point of view which is shared by not a few of our contemporaries who are not members of the Unitarian body. These thinkers combine a keen sense of the important rôle which religion plays in human life with the conviction that the needs which have hitherto been met by conventional theistic religion can be adequately met in the future by devotion to purely human aspirations and ideals.

Humanists of this type differ widely in their at-

---

[2] Babbitt, Irving, *Literature and the American College: Essays in Defence of the Humanities,* 1908; *Humanism and America: Essays on the Outlook of Modern Civilization,* edited by Norman Foerster (New York, 1930).

[3] *Shelburne Essays, 1904–1910; The Greek Tradition* (vols. III and IV): *The Christ of the New Testament; Christ the Word* (1924, 1927).

[4] *Cf.* Reese, Curtis W., *Humanist Sermons* (Chicago, 1927).

titude toward existing social institutions. Some of them believe that a church is still needed, but are convinced that the existing church must be reformed along humanist lines.[5] Others do not think that any specific religious institution is needed. A few are content to retain the word God as a symbol of man's highest social aspirations.[6] Others regard the retention of any term which admits of the conventional theistic interpretation as misleading and dangerous.

When we inquire into the reason for this far-reaching and revolutionary change we find many different factors at work. Some of these factors are intellectual, others practical. In part the change represents a protest against the kind of theology still taught in many churches. This theology is based upon a view of the supernatural which many of our contemporaries believe to be inconsistent with the findings of modern science. It pictures God as a kind of magnified man, with thoughts, purposes, and passions like ourselves, though infinitely more extended in their range, acting upon man directly from time to time as one man would act upon another, and moved to act in one way rather than another by the attitude which his worshippers take toward him. Those who obey his commands and follow his precepts he assists and rewards, if not now, then in the life that is to follow

[5] *E. g.,* Sellars, Roy W., *Religion Coming of Age* (New York, 1928), pp. 286 *f.*

[6] This was the position apparently taken by Professor E. S. Ames in his *Psychology of Religious Experience* (Boston, 1910), p. 313. In his most recent book, *Religion* (Chicago, 1929), he is not content with this subjective position but attributes to God objective cosmic validity (pp. 149–162).

after death. Those who disobey he punishes. Persons trained in the methods of contemporary science find no evidence for the existence of such a God. In the interest of honesty, therefore, they have no option but to reject it.

Others find the practical reasons for rejection most convincing. They tell us that they can no longer believe in God because they find the belief socially demoralizing. It is not simply that God does not exist. It is a good thing that he does not. For, as pictured in the accepted theology, both Catholic and Protestant, he does not deserve our worship. According to this theology God is responsible, directly or indirectly, for all the evil that befalls man. As the author of nature, he is the author of all the evils that come to us through nature—the pain that racks our bodies, the weakness that paralyzes our wills, the futility and ineffectiveness in which so much of the energy which we put into our living culminates. No honorific titles addressed to the author of our being, no repetition of words like "wise" or "loving" or "good," can obscure the fact that the God of historic religion has too often been a God of power rather than of goodness and that in making his bare will the ultimate ground of good man has again and again done violence to his highest instincts alike of justice and of generosity. In bidding farewell once and for all to such a God, these humanists tell us, we open the way for man to be loyal to his own highest ideals, whether nature confirm those ideals or whether she say them nay.

Some moralists put the case against conventional religion even more strongly. It is not simply that faith in God has made acquiescence in things as they are easier. It has put needless obstacles in the way of those who are trying to change them. By making God the champion of the *status quo* it has opposed the august sanctions of revelation to man's legitimate protest against preventable wrongs. In the path of all the great reforms which have won freedom for an oppressed humanity the representatives of organized religion have erected their "Thou shalt not"s until God, instead of being the symbol of humanity's highest aspirations, has become the most powerful single obstacle to their realization. Humanism delivers us from this impossible contradiction. In abolishing God it clears the way for human progress.[7]

The Humanist Assumption Concerning Certainty in Religion

Plausible as are these reasons, convincing as is their appeal to many persons, I do not believe that of themselves they would account for the strength of

[7] This view of religion as a soporific of the conscience, blinding man to the possibilities of present improvement where it does not make him their active opponent, received a powerful reinforcement from the deterministic philosophy of Karl Marx. According to this philosophy we are committed by nature itself to the war of classes. Capitalism is simply one stage in a process of evolution through which society must pass to the dictatorship of the proletariat. For the attainment of this end it is necessary, above all, that the workers organize. Whatever stands in the way of their control, whether it be in state or in church—and to many disciples of Marx the church has seemed quite as dangerous a foe as the state—must be fought with every weapon at their command. I well remember, when a student at Berlin forty years ago, hearing

contemporary humanism had there not been another factor at work. This factor is the assumption already referred to, often unrecognized yet none the less potent, that the only way to gain trustworthy knowledge, and so the certainty that knowledge brings, is through the method of the exact sciences. It is not simply that these sciences have assembled evidence which has led men to question many hitherto accepted beliefs in the field of religion. They have created a temper of mind which has led many people to question whether any trustworthy knowledge concerning God is possible.

There are two senses in which the word "science" may be used. We may use it to express the contrast between beliefs that have been tested and those which are taken over uncritically by suggestion or adopted because of the momentary satisfaction they bring. When we speak of the scientific spirit in this sense we mean the open-minded and conscientious spirit that is unwilling to leave any test unused in its search for the truth. Its marks are comprehensiveness, accuracy, system, impartiality, the critical weighing of all pos-

Bebel, the high priest of the socialism of his day, preaching to a vast audience that filled one of the largest halls in the city the duty of waging unremitting war against the pastor as the man who held the key to the last stronghold in the defense of capitalism against socialism—the home.

The generation that has passed since Bebel has introduced many modifications into the socialist movement. Both in its philosophy and in its practical tactics it has become more reasonable and opportunistic. Socialists have come to see that there is nothing in religion, properly understood, which is the foe of social progress. Indeed, many of them have definitely adopted Christianity as a form of religion which requires for its consistent application the acceptance of the socialist ideal for society. In Communism, however, the old fighting socialism of the Marxian type lives on.

sible alternatives and the adoption of the one which in the light of all the data seems most reasonable. Philosophy is scientific in this sense, in contrast to the untested wisdom of much of our ordinary living. Like every sensible man the philosopher makes probability his guide, but he bases his judgment of what is probable on the widest possible collection of data and, while his method does not yield the mathematical demonstration which is the goal of science, he finds that in many cases it makes it possible for him to reach a very high degree of practical certainty.

The word "science" is also used in a narrower sense to denote the studies which confine their subjects of investigation to those phenomena or aspects of phenomena which admit of exact mathematical test. The physical sciences are examples of this narrower use, and there is a tendency among the representatives of the studies which deal with man, such as psychology, sociology, and history, to regard their work as scientific only in the measure that it conforms to similar tests. This more restricted conception of the function of science is common among humanists, and is in part responsible for their attitude toward religion.

We have seen that the attempt to limit religious faith to the values and meanings which man finds within himself distinguishes the non-theistic form of contemporary humanism from other forms of the humanist movement. Its advocates attempt—needlessly, as we shall try to show—to confine the values and meanings with which religion is concerned to aspects of our own experience of which we have, or can have, exact knowledge. Values they will admit we may still have, provided they are values which we ourselves create. Meanings we may still accept, provided they are meanings which we ourselves discover. But the faith of the older theists in a God who is himself the realization of the highest values and in a purpose which embraces in its transcendent wisdom the conflicting purposes of man, this, it is said, we may no longer hold, not because at any specific point science has disproved what faith asserts, but because the methods through which modern science has won its successes lead us to conclude that the entire enterprise on which religious men have been engaged is a futile one. We may have certainty still, but only within the limits which science sets. Any certainty which goes beyond this—such as the religious man desires and which he once believed himself to possess—we must abandon forever.[9]

It is this assumption as to the limits of possible certainty in religion that we propose to investigate in this book, and the first step in our inquiry is to

[9] It would not be fair to Professor Dewey to class him as a Humanist, since his dominant interest moves along other lines than those of contemporary Humanism. Yet there is much in his recent Gifford lectures on the "Quest for Certainty" which is congenial to the Humanist contention. Writing on the immemorial subject of man's quest of certainty, he tells us that we have failed in the past because we have tried to be sure of too much; we have wanted a God who was the realization of our own highest ideals. This attempt to unite the ideal and the real in ultimate being is the cardinal mistake not only of the historic religions but of the philosophies by which these religions have been influenced.

The true object of religious faith, according to Professor Dewey, is not some absolute God who realizes in Himself the ideal of perfection, but "the possibilities of nature and associated liv-

determine what we mean by certainty and why we
need it.

2. WHAT IT MEANS TO BE SURE

What Is Meant by Certainty

What then do we mean by certainty and why is it
important for us to have it? There are certain current misconceptions on this subject which it will be
well to clear up at the outset.

Certainty is a term which describes an aspect of
consciousness which is present in greater or less degree in different people. It is a state of confidence in
which the mind has come to rest in definite conclusions. These conclusions may be made the basis either
of further thought or of further action. Ordinarily,
though not always, they refer to something outside
ourselves. They have to do either with objects that
are believed to be real or with explanations which are
believed to be true. One may be sure of a fact or of a
person, of a theory or of an ideal, and one's way of
reaching certainty will differ accordingly. But cer-

ing" as they are unfolded to us in our experience of life from day
to day. Such natural religion—the only type of religion appropriate to man, as modern science has enabled us to understand him—
will associate "with its devotion to the ideal, piety toward the actual." It will not be "querulous with respect to the defects and
hardships of the latter, but accepting what it offers with all its
limitations, be thankful for the possibilities it opens to us." Nature, in a word, "may not be worshipped as divine even in the
sense of the intellectual love of Spinoza. But nature, including
humanity, with all its defects and imperfections, may evoke heart-
felt piety as the source of ideals, of possibilities, of aspiration in
their behalf, and as the eventual abode of all attained goods and
excellencies."—*The Quest for Certainty* (New York, 1929), pp.
300, 301, 306.

tainty is always certainty of something and, for the moment, carries its own evidence within itself.

In this combination of inward conviction with outward reference, certainty is like happiness. Both describe something that happens in us, but neither can be understood without reference to the conditions which produce and maintain it. Happiness is happiness in something and can be understood only in the light of some correlative, work or play or love or beauty. In like manner, certainty is certainty of something—a truth to be believed or a reality to be experienced. Neither certainty nor happiness is an end in itself. Each comes to us, when it comes, as an incident in a larger quest—certainty as we follow after truth or reality, happiness as we use our faculties in some worthy or interesting pursuit, love some fellow-creature, or contemplate some beautiful object. Each is to be valued not primarily for its own sake but as an indication that a larger end has been attained.

Some Current Misconceptions

This reminder will help us to understand the misconceptions, already referred to, which tend to confuse our view of the true function of certainty.

One of these current misconceptions is the confusion of certainty with dogmatism. Because there are many people who refuse to submit their beliefs to criticism it does not follow that it is never possible to reach a certainty which will stand the most rigorous tests. There is an unreasoning certainty—the result of credulity or of prejudice—which rejects criticism. There is also a reasoned certainty to which one is led by the strictest methods of science. The child or the savage will believe whatever you tell him till experience has taught him to distrust you. But the mature man welcomes the opportunity to test his beliefs, and if he says he is sure of anything he means that at some point the testing has already taken place.

A second misconception is the confusion of certainty with full, or even with accurate, knowledge. To be sure does not mean to be infallible. To say that I am certain of a thing does not mean that I know all about it, or even that I know what I know with exactness. A child knows its father, certainly, but neither fully nor accurately. To be certain means simply that, at the time, one has confidence that one is in touch with reality and experiences the satisfaction that assured conviction brings to a mind harassed by doubt. Subsequently the form which the conviction first assumed may be shown to be inadequate and to need supplement or even revision. While it lasts, it gives definiteness to thinking and releases energy for action.

Both misconceptions have a common root, namely, the confusion of certainty with changelessness. To be sure of a thing does not mean that the account that I am able to give of it at the present time will never at any point need to be revised. But it does mean, if my certainty is to be trustworthy and not misleading, that there will be something that lasts, something that gives continuity to my experience and unity to my thought. The consciousness of this continuity, with the confidence which it brings into living and acting, is what we shall here mean by certainty.

Certainty Not Inconsistent with Change

We may illustrate the possibility of a certainty which persists in spite of change by the scientist's attitude toward nature,—the realm in which exactness is at once most necessary and most possible. Nature does not mean to the physicist to-day just what it meant to his predecessors of a generation ago, nor does he expect that it will mean to his successors in all respects what it means to him to-day. But when he speaks of nature he is none the less sure that he is dealing with a reality of which he has definite and trustworthy knowledge, and there are some things he can tell you about man's relation to nature which he is confident will not need to be revised. He is certain that there is an order in nature which makes it possible, within limits, to predict how and when things will happen. He is certain that man has the capacity to learn something worth while about that order and to transmit what he has learned to others. He is certain that the way in which this knowledge is to be gained is through an open-minded approach to all the available data, their systematic collection, comparison, and analysis, and the testing of the provisional conclusions reached by repeated experiment. He is certain that the concerted labors of the past have laid a foundation on which he can confidently build, and even while he criticises his predecessors in detail he is conscious that he is standing on a platform which they have raised. He is certain, finally, that there is still more to be learned, and that failure in any specific instance is no reason for doubt that, within the field he has chosen for his study, knowledge will be possible at last.[10]

So the word "nature" becomes for the scientist the symbol of a reality of which he has trustworthy, though partial, knowledge. How different the meaning which "nature" has for a modern astronomer like Eddington or a modern physicist like Millikan from what it had for Aristotle, or, to come closer home, for Sir Isaac Newton. All the discoveries of modern physics; all the new insights of modern chemistry; everything that has been learned by astronomers about light years and solar systems, by biologists about protoplasm and species, has been taken up into the meaning of the word. Yet the reality which the word signifies is the same reality of which the men of Aristotle's day and of Newton's had firsthand experience, and that which they found in it to fascinate and to instruct—order, usefulness, discipline, beauty —is as real to us to-day as it was to them.

What is true of the certainty of science is still more true of the certainty of common life. We are constantly revising our ideas both about persons and

[10] It is important to remember this in view of the revolutionary changes which have taken place in the theories of modern physics and astronomy. When one reads the writings of men like Millikan and Eddington it is natural for the layman to conclude that all is in a state of flux and to overlook the solid basis of assured conviction upon which the elaborate theories of modern physical science have been reared.

about principles without on that account losing confidence in their essential trustworthiness. To say that I am sure of my friend does not mean that I shall always think of him in the same way, or that there is not much to be learned through our daily intercourse that will make him mean more to me next year than he does this year. So to say that I am sure that love is the supreme excellence does not mean that my man's idea of love is the same that I had while I was a child, or that there are not new lessons to be learned about love which will make the word carry new and richer meanings.[11]

If this be true of the certainty of science and of that of common life, how much more must it be true of the certainty of religion. For in religion we are brought face to face with ultimate reality, and this in the most personal way. In religion we are dealing with the living God who is continually communicating his will to men in so far as they are able to re-

[11] The elusive character of many of our value judgments and the extent to which they are affected by the personal equation has led many thinkers to restrict the term "fact" to objects and happenings in the physical world, and to discount the whole realm of value as essentially subjective and untrustworthy. But it needs only superficial observation to show that this conclusion is misleading. In our thinking we distinguish between fact and value. In our own persons they are inseparably connected. We cannot describe what we mean by a person without using such words as good or bad, trustworthy or false, lovable or repugnant. If men did not believe that there was something inherent in the object to which they are attached that deserved the esteem with which they regard it, personal devotion would be impossible, and even the human loves and loyalties on which the humanists base their faith in the coming of a better social order would lack their rational justification. Our museums, too, would soon go out of business, for there would be no reason for preferring the workmanship of a Phidias or of a Rembrandt to the last picture or statue turned out by some modern painter or sculptor who had turned to art not because he loved it but for a living.

ceive it. But man is growing day by day in knowledge, in character, in experience. How impossible then that his idea of God should not be changing to correspond with his enlarging insight. Just because God is the living God, ever at work in his universe, his relation to his worshippers must be constantly changing, and this changing relationship must be reflected in their thought of him. The surer they are of him, the more certain they are that they are dealing with objective reality and not simply with their own subjective moods, the more inevitable will be those adjustments through which their appreciation of the perennial values of life maintains its continuity in the face of an enlarging experience.

So the word "God," like the word "nature," becomes to the worshipper the symbol of a reality of which we have trustworthy, but partial knowledge. Some things the word "God" means to us to-day that it has always meant: superiority, majesty, authority, worshipfulness; others that it has never meant before —things that have entered into our thought of God because of what science has been telling us about the world God has made and because of what history has been telling us about the men and women who have been concerned in its making; and there are other things still to be learned about God that are known by no living man—things which the future holds in store for those who in humility and yet in confidence keep their spirits responsive to the new knowledge which is still to come.

For this reason religious men have always come

back to personality as the most fitting symbol by which to describe God, since personality as we know it in ourselves gives us our most familiar example of a continuity which persists in spite of change. What word, therefore, so well fitted as personality to express the combination of a present reality of definite character and activities with a future of limitless possibility? And it is just this sense of limitless possibility which is central in the religious man's thought of God.

Certainty then, whether it be the certainty of science or that of religion, is not inconsistent with humility, or with open-mindedness, or with growth. Indeed, as we understand it better, we shall come to see that it is the indispensable condition of all three.

3. WHAT CERTAINTY CONTRIBUTES TO EFFECTIVE LIVING

How Certainty Contributes to Progress

This discussion of the nature of certainty will help to make clear to us why we need it. We need it because it is an indispensable tool in the business of living. More particularly we need it because it is the necessary pre-condition of progress, of fellowship, and of happiness.

We need certainty because it is the necessary condition of progress. Progress involves change, but it is change which takes certainty for granted. When we speak of progress we assume some fixed point by which we measure change. Without this, change be-

comes meaningless motion. We call these fixed points
standards or ideals. No feature of our contemporary life, therefore, should cause greater concern
than the growing uncertainty as to ideals. If we are
to make progress in the things that matter most, we
must have some definite conviction as to the presup-
positions from which we start. However little we may
know of the goal toward which we are moving, we
must know the direction in which we wish to go. The
wise man needs to be sure of his ground not because
he wants to stand still but because he wishes to go
forward.

Religion in the past has furnished men with such a
goal. In making them acquainted with God it provided them with a standard which gave direction to
their activity. For God has meant to his worshippers
in every age the reality that expressed their highest
ideal. Contemplating God, as he was pictured to
them in sacred Scriptures or interpreted by living
prophets, they have become conscious of their own
imperfection and, in the effort to realize the task
which he has laid upon them, have become critical of
existing conditions in their own lives and in society at
large. So religion, in making men certain of God,
has made progress possible.[14]

How Certainty Promotes Fellowship

Again we need certainty because it is the necessary
condition of fellowship. When man acquired convic-

[14] *Cf.* Brown, W. Adams, *Beliefs That Matter* (New York,
1928), p. 17.

tions he ceased to be an animal and became a personality. In the measure that he has learned to share convictions he has ceased to be an isolated individual and become a member of society. The possession of common convictions transforms men from independent and separate personalities into families, states, and churches. We need convictions which we can share not simply for the personal satisfaction which the sharing may give us as private individuals, but because of the affections and the sympathies which common conviction makes possible. The great loves and the great friendships have been between people who have had something worth while to share, some great cause that justified sacrifice, some enduring object that called forth worship, some controlling loyalty which inspired discipleship. Loss of conviction, therefore, is the most serious thing that can happen to a society, for unless the lost conviction is speedily replaced by a better, the entire edifice will disintegrate and chaos will be the result.

That is why the present eclipse of religious faith is so disturbing. In losing God men are losing more than a particular belief. They are losing the standards that until yesterday gave definiteness to their views on art and on politics, on education and on morals. Where this loss occurs fellowship in any large sense becomes increasingly difficult, for men have no longer anything worth while to share.

Mr. Lippmann cannot be accused of being unduly prejudiced in favor of the traditional religion. Yet in the book already quoted he gives a vivid picture of the disaster which may follow its loss. Speaking for those intellectuals who, like himself, "are perplexed by the consequences of our own irreligion," he tells us that when they "put their feelings into words they are likely to say that having lost their faith they have lost the certainty that their lives are significant." The modern man

"may be very busy with many things, but he discovers one day that he is no longer sure they are worth doing. He has been much preoccupied; but he is no longer sure he knows why. He has become involved in an elaborate routine of pleasures; and they do not seem to amuse him very much. He finds it hard to believe that doing any one thing is better than doing any other thing, or, in fact, that it is better than doing nothing at all. It occurs to him that it is a great deal of trouble to live, and that even in the best of lives the thrills are few and far between. He begins more or less consciously to seek satisfactions, because he is no longer satisfied, and all the while he realizes that the pursuit of happiness was always a most unhappy quest. . . . And then, surveying the flux of events and the giddiness of his own soul, he comes to feel that Aristophanes must have been thinking of him when he declared that 'Whirl is King, having driven out Zeus.' "[15]

How Certainty Enriches Life

This quotation suggests a third reason why we need certainty. We need it because it is the key to inner peace. The worst enemy of an effective life is fear, and uncertainty is the prolific parent of fear. Fear is always concentrating on the thing that may happen and so prevents us from fixing our attention upon the thing that is happening now. By its antic-

[15] *Op. cit.*, pp. 3–4.

ipation of future disaster it robs us of the gifts which to-day may bring. There is only one way to put this enemy to rout, and that is to lay hold on an enduring good of which no future happening can rob us.

Religion in the past has presented men with such a good when it offered them God. In God they found something secure on which they could count, something sublime to which they could look up. Having this, they possessed the conditions of permanent happiness.

Our psychiatrists well understand the health-giving effect of settled conviction, and for this reason many of them are turning to religion for help in dealing with the morbid states which their diagnosis reveals. When one considers the kind of life that many people are living to-day, a life in which they pass from excitement to excitement, without achieving any dominant loyalty, one cannot but be struck by the fact that their complete loss of certainty as to ultimate reality has had moral as well as intellectual consequences. Mr. Lippmann is not the only one of our contemporaries who is reminding us of this. Bertrand Russell, trying to account for the cynicism of many young people to-day, finds its explanation in the absence of any absolute to which they may give their loyalty.[16] And Professor Dewey, remarking upon

[16] "To the sophisticated youth of the West all this ardor (*i. e.*, the ardor felt by the young men of Russia, of India, and of China) seems a trifle crude. He is firmly persuaded that having studied everything impartially he has seen through everything and that there is nothing remarkable beneath the visiting moon." Even

the loss of individuality in contemporary democracy, is led to a similar diagnosis.[17] A view of life which has as its inevitable consequence the destruction of the conditions of effective living seems of questionable value.

To sum up, we need certainty because it is the condition of effective living. A life that lacks definite commitment is an ineffective life, and indecision is the inevitable result of the loss of assured conviction. The people to whom life has meant most have been people who have been most convinced that they possessed something so excellent that for its sake life

truth ceases to interest him since it is no longer "absolute, eternal, and superhuman." And the same is true of the other ideals to which in the past men have given unquestioning loyalty—religion, country, progress, beauty.—"Why Is Modern Youth Cynical?" *Harper's Magazine*, May, 1930, pp. 721, 723.

[17] "The significant thing is that the loyalties which once held individuals, which gave them support, direction and unity of outlook on life, have well nigh disappeared. In consequence individuals are confused and bewildered. It would be difficult to find in history an epoch so lacking in solid and assured objects of belief, and approved ends of action as is the present. Stability of individuality is dependent upon stable objects to which allegiance formerly attached itself."—*Individualism, Old and New*, II. "The Lost Individual," *The New Republic*, February 5, 1930, p. 294.

Interesting light is thrown on the relativist's contention that a chief obstacle to radical experimentation is the absolutist faith which is fostered by an inherited religion by the fact that the people in our day who have carried social experimentation to most extreme lengths are people who hold most tenaciously to an absolutist philosophy. Economic necessity is a grim substitute for the personal God of theistic faith, but it may fulfil a similar function in nerving the will to disagreeable tasks. There is no stimulus to difficult achievement like the assurance that the forces of the universe are on your side. This assurance the philosophy of Karl Marx makes possible to his followers. Like Calvin when he burned Servetus, or John Knox when he discoursed to Queen Mary on the monstrous regiment of women, they are conscious of being agents of the power to which the future belongs. What if individuals perish, if a whole class must be suppressed by force, if in the end the people come to their own!

itself were well lost. Losing themselves in some great cause they have found freedom to be their best selves, and with this freedom they have won happiness and inner peace.

There would seem to be room then in our modern world for a faith which, while cordially welcoming the new knowledge which modern science brings, still lays hold upon some reality, supremely excellent, which outlasts change.

Yet the tragedy of the present situation consists in this, that at the very time when positive religious conviction seems most needed it is becoming most difficult to attain. There was never a day when more people were eager for definite guidance in the business of living; never a day when their natural helpers seemed more at a loss.

4. Where Certainty Is Needed in Religion

Wrong Reasons for Desiring Certainty in Religion

We have already called attention to the fact that some of our contemporaries are not disturbed by the passing of the old religious certainty. Indeed, far from regretting it, they consider it something to be thankful for. And it is not difficult to understand the reason for their attitude. Not all certainty is of the right kind, nor are the reasons that lead men to desire it always to be commended. Lazy people wish for certainty not in order that they may think better but in order that they may be relieved of the necessity of thinking at all. Timorous people cling tenaciously to old beliefs in the face of evidence which seems to others to disprove them because they are unwilling to face the pain and responsibility of change. What is more unfortunate still, autocratic people, dreading the consequences of the misuse of freedom in others, try to impose their own beliefs on society at large and condemn any departure from conventional standards as immoral. All these motives operate in the field of religion and their effects are often disastrous. No impartial student of the history of religion but must recognize that the certainty which religious people have claimed in the past has often been narrowing rather than enlarging. It has bred intolerance. It has fostered mental inertia. It has been the authoritarian's most trusted weapon in his battle against freedom. In particular it has brought with it an easy acquiescence in things as they are that has made reform difficult, often impossible. But man was not meant to acquiesce. He grows in maturity as he questions his beliefs. It is his uncertainty, not his certainty, that distinguishes him from all other creatures and makes him a resourceful being. No account of the history of religion will do justice to all the facts which does not have a place of honor for many who have been called heretics and rebels. Doubt is the price which the free man pays for his convictions.

But because the motives which lead men to wish for certainty are sometimes unworthy it does not follow that certainty is not to be desired. It will be a sad commentary on our modern education if, after all the labor that has been put into the quest of truth, the best that a teacher can pass on to a pupil interested in the ultimate questions is an "I do not know!" Of what value is our experience if we have nothing to leave to those who come after us? The more we believe in freedom, the more firmly we are convinced of the right of each individual to try his own experiments and to make his own tests for himself, the more we must desire to reach some fixed principles on which we can agree and upon which we can lay a foundation from which we can build higher.

Fields in Which Discrimination Is Needed

It will help us to discriminate between what is essential and what is unessential in our quest of a dependable faith if we remind ourselves of some of the questions that play a great rôle in contemporary discussion on which many religious people have come to feel that certainty is not necessary. Some of these things have to do with ourselves, some of them with other people, some of them with the world in which we live.

Thus it would be very interesting to know how the world has come to be and how long it has lasted. It would be interesting to know whether the view of the atom which is held by modern physics is likely to maintain itself as a trustworthy explanation of the ultimate units of matter or whether it will yield to other explanations, as the older theories have yielded before it. It would be interesting to know whether Einstein is right in his doctrine of relativity, and still more interesting to some of us to understand exactly what that doctrine is. But it is not necessary for our practical living for us to know the answer to any of these questions. We might accept any one of many possible answers and still find ourselves facing similar alternatives and forced to decide between issues of the same kind.

In like manner, it would be very interesting to know what lies beyond us in the future, how long the earth is to last, and what form life will ultimately assume when those revolutionary changes have taken place in our planet to which the geologists bid us look forward. We should greatly like to know what is to happen during the intermediary period which will be the subject of the historian of the future; what is to be the fate of our country and of the other nations with which we are now associated; what are to be the relations between Orient and Occident, between the white man and the black, the yellow race and the brown. Will democracy hold its own against the challenge of imperialism, or will we evolve some new form of government different from any known to us as yet? Are those right who tell us that there are other wars to come, or have we in the League of Nations an instrument that will really bring about universal peace in our time? It would be very interesting if we could have an answer to these questions, and it would be definitely helpful if we could have an answer to some of them. But it is not necessary that we should have an answer so far as our present duty is concerned. The issues that face us to-day lie closer at hand and the questions on which we must have certainty, if possible, are of a more intimate and personal character.

Finally, there is much that it would be interesting to us to know about ourselves. We should like to know how far we are creatures of our past and how far new creatures, inexplicable by our antecedents; what part is played in our decisions by conscious thought, what part by sub-conscious influences; how body and spirit are related and in what sense each depends upon the other; what part is played by heredity and what by environment in making us what we are; which of the competing theories of the psychologists we ought to believe when they tell us contradictory things about ourselves. All these are questions which are most interesting and important and some day we shall know more about them than we do to-day. But this knowledge is not essential to us now, provided we can know one or two things about ourselves on which everything turns.

Where Certainty Is Essential in Religion

But there are a few things, a very few, on which certainty is all important because it affects our conduct, and still more our feelings, in the things that matter most. We need to know enough to act rightly in the sphere in which we are personally responsible for action. We need to know enough to give us confidence in those with whom we must co-operate in the common tasks that are beyond our unaided strength. We cannot always be halting between two opinions. We cannot always be waiting for science to report to us the outcome of experiments which have not yet begun. There are regions of life in which action is imperative, where we must choose in this way or in that. There are interests of more than present moment, interests that affect our own lives, interests that affect lives dearer to us than our own; and we need some standard by which to measure them in the right way, some principle of valuation that will make it possible for us to say, and to say with confidence: This is right. That is good. This is honorable. That is beautiful. This is lovely and of good report. And beyond all this there is an area of life where thought fails us, where action is no longer possible, where after the shock of some great sorrow or some paralyzing pain we sit numb and helpless and, raising blind eyes to heaven, cry: O God, if there be a God—if I could only be sure!

It is with issues such as these that religion is concerned; issues on which certainty seems necessary and where at the same time it is so desperately hard to reach; issues which determine our principles of conduct, furnish us with our standard of judgment, define for us the meaning or lack of meaning of life as a whole.

We see now why faith in God must always hold a central place in the religious man's quest of certainty. For God is the name we give to the reality which is most excellent in the universe, the basic fact on which our faith in all other good depends. To have faith in God in the sense in which the theistic religions have understood God, means to be persuaded that there is at the heart of the universe a reality in some true sense akin to man, though infinitely wiser and better, who gives the answer to his ultimate questions, sets the standard for his estimate of value, and with whom a fellowship is possible that gives joy to life, strength for work, and inspiration for high adventure.

It is of course true that this is not the only conception of God which has been held by religious people, or which is held to-day. It is, however, the conception of God which has come to us through the historic tradition, Jewish and Christian, of which we of the Western world are heirs, and it is still the spring of much—many of us would believe, of most— that is precious and inspiring in our lives. We may well take it, then, as a convenient example to use in testing the possible methods of reaching certainty. To be sure of God in the sense in which we shall be using the term in what follows means to be persuaded, not simply that there exists such a reality as the word "God" symbolizes, but that we can recognize God's presence in specific symbols and draw upon him for the wisdom, the power, and the love we need.

Believers in a personal God have differed widely in the way they have conceived God's relation to man, some finding man's kinship to God primarily in his possession of self-consciousness and the power of reflective thought, others in deeper impulses and intuitions which elude exact definition; some seeking God's revelation in extraordinary events of miraculous character, others finding it in the orderly processes of nature and of history. But however they have thought of God in detail, it has always been of one who reveals himself in definite experiences and whose presence is evidenced by the graces of faith and hope and love. When one realizes what such a faith may mean for life, one does not wonder that those who possess it regard it as the one thing needful.

The Importance of Taking Time

We are not at fault then in wanting certainty in religion. The trouble with most of us is that we are not willing to wait for it or to fulfil the necessary conditions for acquiring it. We want our certainty as the commuter wants his breakfast—ready at our call. If we cannot get it in that way, we are tempted to give it up altogether.

Yet that is not the attitude we take toward the other good things of life. The things that we prize most in ourselves do not come without effort. They have to be won by concentration and sacrifice in the course of the discipline of life. This is true of freedom. It is true of happiness. It is true of character. Certainty is no exception. We have to work for it. And because we have to work for it, and often to wait for it, it is all the more precious when it comes.

We are ready enough to recognize this in other matters in which we are interested. Our knowledge of the physical universe has come to us in this way. Yet we do not question its trustworthiness or its availability. We honor our men of science just because they limit their hypotheses so narrowly and test them so rigorously. We do not trust their conclusions less because there is a wide area in which they profess ignorance or because, even in those regions in which they are agreed as to the facts, they differ as to their explanations. We know that progress in knowledge is won at the cost of repeated experiment and we are content to take what science can give us now and to wait for fuller light by and by.

It is so with the certainties of common life—our loyalty to institutions and our trust in friends. Here, too, convictions are won slowly and often at the cost of many mistakes. But these facts do not destroy our confidence that in the end certainty will be possible. For we have found it to be so in our own experience. There are areas of life in which we have won convictions which repeated experiment has served only to confirm, and we do not doubt that these areas can be extended if we follow the methods that are appropriate.

Why should we suppose it to be otherwise in religion? Here, if anywhere, we should expect that certainty must be attained step by step, since in religion we have to do with the reality of all realities most difficult to grasp in its entirety. The object of religion is not only the greatest of realities but also the most active. Wherever we turn, in nature, in history, in our own lives, we find God at work, and for that very reason our ideas of him must be constantly changing. Yet the fact that our thought of God is changing is no more a reason for questioning our certainty of his existence or the reality of his revelation than the fact that our thought of the friends we trust is changing is a reason for doubting our certainty of them. If our beliefs about God never needed to be revised, it would be the surest proof that it is not really God with whom we have to do.

The Issue Raised by Contemporary Humanism

If humanists were content to remind us of this fact we should only be grateful to them, for it is a reminder of which we are constantly in need. It is easy to identify our transient beliefs with eternal reality and in our eagerness to hold fast some past insight to lose the new revelation which lies at our door. But when some humanists go farther and deny the possibility of our knowing God in any form, they leave the assured ground of fact and become dogmatists in their turn.

This is the more discouraging because there is nothing in their own philosophy, when properly understood, to require this attitude. We have seen that they differ from the earlier representatives of materialistic naturalism in being unwilling to exclude from the real world meanings and values which do not admit of exact quantitative analysis. They recognize in their philosophy of life insights which come through immediate intuition. They believe that words like beauty and goodness and love correspond to realities in nature. They would organize life so as to give these realities effective expression. But they think that this should be done only within limits which science can control, a field which they believe to be confined to the human values and meanings which are accessible to us as men. They do not deny that, within the limits thus set, our final conviction as to the trustworthiness of the standards to which we give assent must be won through an act of personal faith, not unlike that through which the great masters of religion have won their conviction as to the supreme reality in which they believed. But when the faith of an Augustine or of a Phillips Brooks reaches beyond the human values and meanings revealed in our relations to our fellowmen and rests at last in a Cosmic Friend whom religion calls God, they part company with us. At this point, they tell us, we have passed beyond the limits of attainable certainty.

It is not easy to see why they should do this. It cannot be because the object of religious faith has qualitative as well as quantitative character, for within the field of human relationships humanists admit the trustworthiness of qualitative judgments. It cannot be because the method by which we win our certainty in religion involves an appeal to a faith which outruns the possibility of exact mathematical demonstration, for even exact science, as we have seen, rests in the last analysis upon the legitimacy of such a faith. Two possible explanations remain which invite further investigation. One is that the religious man has failed to define the object of his faith in such a way as to make possible the continuous reinterpretation which is the condition of all progress in knowledge. The other is that he has not been willing to submit that object to the tests that are available within the field where by common consent these tests apply.

It may be freely admitted that in the past religious thinkers have often laid themselves open to both these criticisms. They have identified their belief in God with particular scientific theories as to his relation to the world and to man and have claimed for the latter the finality which rightly belongs only to the former. They have professed access to sources of knowledge not open to ordinary people and, relying upon these, have been unwilling to submit their conclusions to the tests through which belief is validated in other realms.

But because in the past religious people have made these mistakes it does not follow that, when faith in God is rightly defined and the conditions of its testing have been rightly determined, it cannot be shown to be as reasonable as any of the other basic convictions by which we regulate our lives. In the chapters that follow we shall try to show that this faith is indeed a reasonable faith.

CHAPTER II

WAYS OF REACHING CERTAINTY

1. How Convictions Are Born and How They Maintain Their Life.

   What Psychology Can Tell Us About the Origin of Belief—The Physical Basis of Belief—The Influence of Suggestion—The Emotional Factor in Belief—The Importance of the Personal Equation—The Contribution of Symbols to Common Conviction.

2. Why Untested Belief Is Not Enough.

   How Reasoned Conviction Differs from Rationalization—What It means to Validate a Belief—Reasons Which Make Retesting Necessary.

3. Four Ways of Testing Belief.

   Ways of Testing Belief—Need of Using Each in the Right Way.

4. How the Nature of the Belief to Be Tested Determines the Method to Be Used in Testing It.

   How the Scientist's Use of the Four Ways Differs from that of the Religious Man—Is Revelation a Fifth Way?

One of the most important contributions of modern psychology is its disclosure of the non-rational factors which enter into the making of our beliefs. Among these are our physical constitution, the suggestions that come to us from others, and our emotional states. So far-reaching is the influence of these factors that there are persons who regard reason as negligible in the production of our beliefs and restrict its services to the defense of their validity when once they have been adopted.

It is necessary then to distinguish between the causes which produce our religious convictions and the reasons which justify us in continuing to hold them. These reasons may be of four different kinds. We may rely upon the testimony of others who have believed before us. We may find a sufficient reason for our faith in the immediate satisfaction which it brings. We may justify our belief by showing that it is consistent with what we know in other realms. We may act on the assumption that our belief is true and find that the results justify our confidence.

These four ways of validating belief may be called, respectively, the way of authority, the way of intuition, the way of reasoning, and the way of experiment. Scientists and religious people alike use all four in ways that are appropriate to their dominant purpose. Revelation is often distinguished as a fifth way but, when rightly defined, will be found to include and to unify all the other ways.

1. How Convictions Are Born and How They Maintain Their Life

What Psychology Can Tell Us About the Origin of Belief

In defining what is at stake in religious certainty, we saw that the issue on which everything turns is the possibility of winning an assurance of the existence of a wise and loving God. Faith in such a God gave unity and meaning to the life of our predecessors. The loss of this faith has made the lives of many of our contemporaries ineffective, lonely, and unhappy. For us Twentieth Century people, therefore, the possibility of winning certainty in religion will depend upon our finding reasons which will justify us in continuing to hold this faith when challenged or which will enable us to recover it when lost. We shall be helped in our search for such reasons by reminding ourselves how convictions arise and how they live.

Psychologists tell us that the process of acquiring a belief is in part a non-rational process. Many factors enter into the making of our beliefs besides the reasons which we give to justify them, and this fact affects our problem of certainty in important, often in perplexing, ways. Among the non-rational factors that affect belief are our physical constitution, the suggestions that come to us from others, and the complicated system of sentiments and dispositions, likes and dislikes, which we call our temperament.

49

The Physical Basis of Belief

Basic for an understanding of our present life is the intimate connection which exists between body and mind. Everything that we do and everything that we experience has a physical basis. Our thoughts are no exception. When we are in good physical health we are apt to see more clearly and to reason more accurately than when we are racked by pain, and there are physical conditions which make correct thinking impossible and in many cases put a stop to thinking altogether.

The intimate connection between body and mind has long been a matter of common knowledge. But modern medical science has enormously increased both the amount and the accuracy of this knowledge. It has proved the connection between our conscious life and its physical basis not only in general but in detail. We now know that there are definite centres in the brain that control definite phases of our thought and of our activity. A clot of blood in one part of the brain may deprive a man of the use of a limb; a similar clot in another part of the brain may turn a sane man into an idiot. Side by side with our processes of thought there are physical processes that are going on in ways of which we are largely unconscious, and if anything goes amiss with one set of these processes there is certain to be trouble with the other.

The discovery of the dependence of our mental processes on physical conditions has been a source of perplexity to many thinkers. It has seemed to rob man of his freedom and to reduce him to an automaton. But there is nothing in the facts as we know them that shuts us up to such a conclusion. If God is the God of the whole world, as the teachers of the great religions have affirmed, nature as well as man is the sphere of his influence. There is no reason, therefore, why among the factors which God uses in the accomplishment of his will for man the laws of the body should not be included. We are not less sure that the messages which come to us from those we love convey a spiritual meaning because they are transmitted through the bodily channels of speech and touch. Why then should our thought of God be any less trustworthy or any less satisfying because it is physically conditioned?

Whatever the relation between our thoughts and the nerve processes which accompany and condition them, it is a reciprocal relation. If a diseased body can warp and pervert our thinking, right thoughts can often bring stimulus and healing to the body. Among the gifts for which religious people have most confidently looked to their religion, health is one of the most recurrent. Christian Science is only the latest of many examples of the healing quality of religious faith.

The Influence of Suggestion

A second non-rational factor that enters into the making of religious belief is suggestion, by which we mean the influence, deliberate or unconscious, which is exerted upon us by the example of our neighbors. One of the most potent influences in the development of personality is imitation, and imitation plays a part in the formation of our habits of thought as well as of our ways of action. No one of us initiates his own beliefs any more than he chooses his own parents. We acquire our beliefs as we acquire our manners,—by contagion. We were born into a world where we found people already believing and we made their beliefs our own. We believed what our parents believed, or what the children with whom we played told us, or what our teachers or our minister taught us. These beliefs were concerned with many matters: with our home, with our school, with our country, with our church, with our neighbors and our friends. Whatever they were, it never occurred to us to doubt them. They were just as much a part of the structure of the world in which we lived as the ground on which we trod.

But once again there is nothing in this fact that ought to surprise or disturb us. Where there is so much to be known, it would be impossible to make progress at all unless there were some way by which the inheritance of past generations could be transmitted to their successors. The raw material of all education is the inherited beliefs of the past. We do not attempt to verify all those beliefs, nor is it necessary that we should. We have other things to do besides think. We must work; we must enjoy; we must love; we must worship. And we cannot do any one of these effectively if we are always stopping to ask whether it is wise to do so. The sensible man reserves his thoughts for the most important matters and, for the rest, relies upon the accumulated wisdom of the past.

Nevertheless, this attitude of acquiescence must not be carried too far. The suggestions that come to us from our neighbors are not all helpful. Sometimes the things which they ask us to believe are not true. Often the things which they wish us to do are not advisable. If belief were a purely academic matter, we might without great danger accept what others tell us. But some of our thoughts have practical consequences, often of far-reaching importance.

The Emotional Factor in Belief

It is at the point where belief affects conduct that a third non-rational factor makes its presence felt,— the emotional factor. Good and evil, right and wrong, God and Christ, salvation and the church, do not meet us simply in the form of abstract propositions to be debated in the classroom or the discussion group, but in the form of causes to be espoused or leaders to be followed. If I commit myself to this alternative rather than that, it may mean sacrifice and loneliness, the loss of friends or of position, in extreme instances persecution and death. My conviction may become a determining factor in the entire ordering of my life and, what is still more important, in the life of others. Many a man who could endure hardship for himself shrinks from it for his

wife and children. Yet the choices which he must make
day by day may sooner or later involve consequences
which force him to face this issue.

It is not strange that when decisions have such
momentous effects our feelings should be deeply engaged. No contribution of psychology to the understanding of the personal life is more illuminating
than what it has taught us about the part which emotion plays in our thinking as well as in our acting.
This emotional factor is most in evidence in the beliefs that have to do with persons. Here our likes and
dislikes are especially deep-rooted and persistent.
And what is true of human persons is true in equal
measure of the supreme person with whom religion
has to do. My belief in God will express itself in
sentiments of reverence and gratitude which lead me
to worship, as well as in the sentiment of loyalty that
leads me to obey.[1]

The Importance of the Personal Equation

Persons differ greatly in the extent to which they
are influenced by their emotions and in the direction

[1] Unless we take account of this emotional factor in religious
belief we cannot understand the attitude of a man like Mr. Bryan
in his opposition to evolution. To him it was not a question of
what had happened æons ago when our first ancestor was created,
but of what was happening in America to-day. Others might accept evolution as a commonplace of science. To Mr. Bryan and
his friends in Tennessee it seemed fraught with the most disastrous
consequences. It led men to question the existence of God, the
trustworthiness of the Bible, the possibility of a new creative experience brought about through faith in God, the Father Al-
mighty. They thought it intolerable that the teaching of a doctrine
which entailed such disastrous consequences should be allowed in

which the influence takes. The psychologists have
names for the tendencies which lead us to feel in different ways. They call them sentiments and dispositions. These tendencies, which together make up
what we call temperament, affect our belief in important ways. They give it a certain character which
makes it peculiarly our own. Much as beliefs re-
semble one another, there is always a personal equation which, like the overtone in music, gives its dis-
tinctive character to what is believed. For no two
men does the same word mean exactly the same thing.

This personal equation affects both the nature of
the belief and the method by which it is acquired.
The appeal of different arguments to different people is determined in part by their temperament, and
the conclusions to which they come will vary accordingly. Some people are naturally of an inquiring
disposition and must be able to give a definite reason
for everything they believe. Others, more trustful
by nature, turn to authority for their justification.
Father Tyrrell, himself a natural sceptic, tells in his

the public schools and they were prepared to oppose it by every
means in their power.

Obviously this was not an attitude which could be changed simply by argument as to the findings of science. It was not the
findings of science as such to which Mr. Bryan took exception but
the conclusions which he believed, rightly or wrongly, to follow
from them. Before a hearing for these findings could be had there
must be a change of emotional atmosphere. The fear that inhibits
attention must be removed either by the discovery that evolu-
tionary process and divine creation are not inconsistent or by the
discovery of some substitute for religious faith that will make
life tolerable without it.

On the part played by emotion in determining man's attitude
toward belief, *cf*. Walter Lippmann's suggestive book on *Public
Opinion*, New York, 1922.

autobiography of a Catholic friend[3] who in all his
life had never known what it was to doubt. Persons
of mystical temperament have a capacity for spiritual
vision which makes God the most vivid of all realities
to them, while more matter-of-fact persons have to
win their faith little by little through the comparison
of alternative possibilities. These differences not
only determine the way in which certainty will be
reached, but the relative weight which will be given
to different forms of proof when the conclusions
reached have been challenged.

The influence of the personal equation will vary in
intensity according to the subject matter of the belief. In beliefs about things which can be weighed or
measured, like the height of a person or the tonnage
of a steamer, it is reduced to a minimum. One man's
belief is for all practical purposes the same as every
other man's. In beliefs about subjects which involve
judgments of value, like the character of a person or

---

[3] Father Morris. The following words, written by Father Morris
in his last retreat and quoted in his *Life* by Father J. H. Pollen, S.J.,
will give further light on his character, and confirm the impression
left by the description in the *Autobiography:*

"In all my life as a Catholic, now fully forty-seven years, I cannot remember a single temptation against faith that seemed to me
to have any force. The Church's teaching is before me, as a glorious series of splendid certainties. My mind is absolutely satisfied.
Faith is an unmixed pleasure to me, without any pain, any difficulty, any drawback. . . . I have no private judgment to overcome, and no desire to exercise my private judgment. It is a greater pleasure to receive and possess truth with certainty, than to go
in search of it and to be in uncertainty whether it has been found.
The teaching of the Church is perfectly worthy of God, and it
makes me happy. A declaration or definition of the Holy See is
a real joy to me. So much more of certain and safe possession of
truth."—*Autobiography* of George Tyrrell, Supplement to chap.
XIII, p. 229.

the beauty of a picture, on the other hand, the variable element is at its highest. No two people enjoy and no two worship in exactly the same way.

This variation in the quality of belief is consistent with a high degree of common conviction. While no two members of the same family think exactly alike on all subjects, in a normal home there is a great body of beliefs which all alike share. This body of common conviction is the rock on which family life is built. Without it there could be neither unity nor happiness. And what is true of the family is true in greater or less degree of all the other social groups to which we belong. It is true pre-eminently of the Church.

The Contribution of Symbols to Common Conviction

The presence of a body of common conviction which is consistent with considerable variation in detail explains, among other things, the use of symbols. Symbols are a means by which we are able to express in simple and untechnical form the common insights and loyalties which form the bond of social life. These symbols may be either physical or verbal. Examples of physical symbols are the flag, the ring, and the cross; examples of verbal symbols, the words "God," or "Christ," or "Spirit." These symbols mean different things to different people, yet these differences are consistent with a degree of unity in conviction. No two Americans think of America in quite the same way, yet to every patriotic citizen his country stands for something precious, something which evokes loyalty and justifies sacrifice; and the fact that he thinks, and, what is still more to the point, that he feels, about his country in this way constitutes the bond which unites him with all who think and feel as he does, in spite of the many differences which separate them in other respects.

The loyalties of religion in like manner make room for difference. They express unity in diversity, continuity in change. We have seen that the word "God" does not mean to the men of to-day just what it meant to the men of the sixteenth century, still less what it meant to the men of the tenth century, or of the first. Nevertheless, it means some things which it meant to them, and the things which it meant to them and which it means to us are more important than the things in which we differ.

The same is true of the words "Christ," or "salvation," or "church." They not only express unities, they express difference; and *they express both at the same time*. This fact, rooted in the nature of the personal life, is the condition which makes society possible. Without it we should remain isolated individuals, as separate as the pebbles on the beach.

Two facts concerning these symbols of historic religion have important consequences for our understanding of the religious experience. One is the ease with which they can be separated from the reality to which they point. The other is their capacity for constant reinterpretation.

No fact is more familiar in the history of religion than the worshipper's tendency to identify the object of his faith with the sign through which that object makes its presence known. From this it is only a step to the position where the sign itself is given a potency which is in reality attributable only to the object of its reference. The sacrament that evidences the divine presence becomes a charm by which that presence can be induced at will. The name that was originally designed to suggest the divine majesty acquires a sanctity which makes it dangerous to utter it. The incarnation that was meant to make God's presence more vivid becomes a barrier separating his children from one another.

This confusion of sign and thing signified is the parent of all kinds of narrowness and superstition. The symbol that first made man aware of God's presence in his world becomes a barrier to further insight. Would-be worshippers are warned that they must find God in this way or not at all and every other method of approach to deity is ruled out as illegitimate, if not positively profane.

Fortunately the story of symbolic religion has another side and a happier one. It is true that religious symbols have often divided men, sadly and unnecessarily divided them; but it is no less true that they have quite as often united them. This is due to a second characteristic of symbols which is quite as important. I mean their capacity for constant reinterpretation. Words acquire new meanings as we use them. And what is true of the words that are spoken is true also of the unspoken signs that bring their message to the eye and to the touch.

If it were not for this power of signs to acquire
new meanings progress in knowledge would be impossible, for life is not simply a matter of the intellect but of the whole personality. While we are learning to understand the world in which we live we have
to go on living in it, and for this we need signs which
express the continuity of our experience even while
it is in the process of change.

The existence of these common signs which are in
process of continual reinterpretation raises perplexing problems both for the scientist and for the states-
man. How can we express the things that we hold in
common without doing injustice to the things about
which we disagree? How far can change go without
parting the tie that binds us to the past? These are
questions on which honest men may differ. Yet unless
there is some unity which is consistent with change
there could be no social life in any form.

Thus it appears that the influences which determine belief are extraordinarily complex. Besides
the logical grounds which reason analyzes and the
practical considerations which appeal to our sympathy and to our loyalty, subconscious influences are
operating of which we are largely unaware. Habit
plays its part, and convention, superstition, and
prejudice. Besides all these are the physical influences that are the result of the general condition of
our bodily system. When we are dealing with a subject so personal as certainty, we must take account of
all these influences. It is futile to approach a person
suffering from a diseased brain with an argument.

What he needs is not a logician but a surgeon. So beliefs that are simply the reflection of personal interest or prejudice can rarely be dealt with by reasoning alone. We must penetrate to the deeper causes which are at work and deal with them. A defective syllogism may be corrected by more accurate analysis. An emotional attitude can ordinarily be altered only by one who approaches it with sympathy.

2. WHY UNTESTED BELIEF IS NOT ENOUGH

How Reasoned Conviction Differs from Rationalization

So far we have been studying the natural history of belief. We have seen that in this history non-rational factors play a large and, in many cases, a determining part. But certainty won in this way is an insecure possession. For the factors that have produced it may at any moment destroy it. Fortunately there is another way of reaching certainty which promises surer results, a way in which thought rather than emotion plays the controlling part. Man differs from other living creatures largely in his ability to think logically, in other words in his power to visualize alternative possibilities and to make clear to himself and to others the reasons for his conclusions. Education is concerned largely with developing this power and applying it to constantly wider areas of knowledge and of experience.

This is not an easy thing to do. Among our dislikes, the dislike of being thus disciplined is one of the strongest. In many people, as we have seen, the emotions are much more strongly developed than the intellect. They may pay a certain outward respect to the claims of logic, but it will be a half-hearted allegiance. It is not hard to find plausible reasons for continuing to do or to believe the things that we like, or for refraining from doing or from believing the things that we do not like. Psychologists have a name for this process of finding reasons to justify our likes and our dislikes. They call it rationalization. So common is it and so far-reaching in its effects that many psychologists are inclined to give to logic a subordinate part in the forming of our convictions and to regard most, if not all, of our reasoning as a form of self-sophistication by which we invent plausible reasons for continuing to cherish our preconceived opinions and prejudices.[4]

What It Means to Validate a Belief

There are, however, certain simple tests by which we can distinguish true reasoning from this spurious imitation. One is the test of consistency, another that of permanence, a third that of communicability. A reasoned belief differs from one that is held on emotional grounds, partly in that it is consistent with all the other beliefs that we hold, partly in that it maintains itself in the light of all the new evidence that may be forthcoming, partly in that it can be shared

[4] The late Mr. J. P. Morgan is reported once to have said that every man has two reasons for what he does: a good reason and the real reason.

by others who have tested it for themselves. We call
the result of this testing validation. To say of a belief that it is valid means that after giving full weight
to all the evidence that can be massed against it the
reasons which justify us in continuing to hold it still
retain their force. These reasons need not be new
reasons; they may be, they often are, the same
reasons which originally led to our believing. But our
attitude toward them will have changed. Then we
followed them unthinkingly, without realizing what
we were doing. Now we hold to them because we are
persuaded that, of all possible alternatives, they give
us the soundest basis of confidence. A validated belief is a tested belief, a belief we have consciously
made our own after weighing all the available
evidence.

The process by which our beliefs are tested is
known as logic and the sum of the beliefs which have
stood the test form the subject-matter of the sciences.

These beliefs have to do with objects of two very
different kinds: things that are known to us by sense
perception and can therefore be weighed, and measured, and tabulated, and qualities like goodness and
beauty and honor, which we recognize through our
judgments of value. Science in the technical sense is
concerned with realities of the first kind, art and
ethics with realities of the second. Philosophy attempts a synthesis of all our knowledge and is therefore concerned with both aspects of reality. In philosophy, as in the common knowledge of every day,
we have to do with life as a whole. But philosophy

differs from the knowledge of common life in its critical character. It is tested knowledge, differing from science in the narrow sense only in that it does not exclude from its sources of knowledge those judgments of value which bring meaning into life and express its purposes.

Reasons Which Make Retesting Necessary

There are many reasons which may lead us to submit our inherited beliefs to the retesting of science and of philosophy. But the most common is the discovery of apparently conflicting beliefs, between which we must choose. Sometimes the realization comes to us from without, through contact with those who question the beliefs which we hold; sometimes it comes from within, through some inner conflict within ourselves. We find that there are other standards of conduct than those of our parents, other ways of thinking besides those of our teachers, other ways of worshipping besides that of our minister. The authorities that claim our allegiance do not agree and the time comes when we must take sides. However the realization comes, it is a sobering, sometimes a dismaying, experience. I shall never forget how my heart sank when I first learned that the dictionary is not infallible.

Those who question the beliefs which we hold usually do so for one of two reasons: either because they question the facts on which the belief rests or because they explain them in some other way. Thus a man

may reject the theory of evolution either because he
does not accept the evidence which is cited in proof
of it or because he believes that the evidence can be
accounted for in a different way. In the first case his
challenge may cause us to reconsider the grounds on
which we have accepted the theory. In the second
case it may lead us to reformulate our statement in
the hope of meeting his objection. Where differences
have to do simply with different ways of explaining
the same facts they may often be passed over without
loss. When, however, the difference concerns the
reality believed in, the matter becomes more serious;
and when the facts are not physical simply, like the
size of a house or the date of an event, but involve
judgments of value, like the character of a person or
the worthiness of a cause, the difference grows more
serious. It is a matter of little interest to those of us
who are not astronomers whether the sun is a million
miles from the earth or a hundred million, but what
we think of a candidate for the Presidency will affect
our vote, and what we believe about the needs of
society may determine our choice of a profession. It
is when we face decisions of this kind that we realize
that certainty is not a gift to be enjoyed but a prize
to be won.

3. FOUR WAYS OF TESTING BELIEF

Ways of Testing Belief

There are four ways in which we may test a belief.
All of them have been in use since thought began and

are still in use to-day. Our predecessors in the quest of certainty have used them all and have found each efficacious. Some searchers have followed the beaten track of tradition. They have based their certainty upon their confidence in the wisdom of those who have studied the subject before them. Others have used the scientist's method of classification and analysis. They have assembled all the factors bearing upon the subject of their quest and justified the conclusion to which they have come by its inner consistency with all the data as yet available. Still others have reached their goal by the poet's method, as in some sudden flash of insight they have seen the solution after which thought had wrestled in vain. Others, finally, have made practice their final test. They have lived out their faith and, where that faith had to do with matters of social, as well as individual, reference, they have initiated a process of experiment which has often required for its completion the co-operation of many succeeding generations.

We may call these four ways, for convenience, the way of Authority, the way of Reasoning, the way of Intuition, and the way of Experiment.

All these are methods which we use in dealing with questions which perplex us, and each has its contribution to make. Sometimes our certainty comes to us by the way of authority, sometimes by the way of reasoning, sometimes by the way of intuition, sometimes by the way of experiment. Some convictions we take over at second hand on the testimony of some one we trust or as part of the common heritage of the race; some we win for ourselves by a process of reasoning from the data that are available to the conclusions which seem logically to follow. Some come to us in a flash of insight whose source we are often unable to discover, but which none the less carries irresistible conviction. Still others we hold because we have put them to the test of experiment and found that the results have followed which we expect.[5]

Need of Using Each in the Right Way

All these methods, I repeat, we use in our quest of certainty, and all of them are legitimate as far as they go. Science and philosophy, as well as religion, use them all in ways that are appropriate to their dominant purpose. But we are not always discriminating in our use of them. We put on some one method all the weight of the issue to be tested and, when we find that it is not strong enough to carry it alone, we conclude that we are shut up to uncertainty, although such a conclusion does not necessarily follow. Some tests are valid for some questions and others for others. If we are wise, we shall use each in its proper place.

[5] Professor William P. Montague, in his suggestive book, *The Ways of Knowing* (New York, 1925), adds two other possible methods: the way of sense perception (empiricism) and the way of doubt (scepticism). But careful consideration will show that these are not so much independent methods as reminders of factors that we have to take into account in our use of the other four methods. Sense perception furnishes us with the primary material from which reasoning draws its inferences and to which intuition lends its meaning. Scepticism carries the method of experiment to its ultimate limit by systematically doubting everything that it is possible to doubt. Of that which remains when the test is complete, we may say with confidence, "we know."

Let us take an example from a field which is causing difficulty to some of our religiously-minded contemporaries. Suppose that we wish to know which of the words attributed to Jesus in the Gospels were really spoken by him. How shall we set about resolving this difficulty?

One possible way would be to find some one who was in a position to know and to trust his answer. If Jesus were still alive, we might go to him and ask him whether he had been correctly reported. Since this is not now possible, we might go to the best living authority on his teaching, whatever we conceived that authority to be. If we are Roman Catholics we might go to a priest and ask him to tell us what the church has taught on the subject. If we are Protestants we might go to some New Testament scholar and learn from him what the most competent students of the Gospels believe. And what we learned in these ways we might accept as settling the question for us. This is the simplest and easiest of the paths to certainty—the way of authority.

But it might well be that in a matter of such importance we should be unwilling to take our conclusions at second hand. We might ourselves turn critics and weigh the evidence for ourselves. We might compare the words which were questioned with other words of Jesus of whose authenticity we have no doubt, considering in turn the vocabulary, the style, and the world of thought in which the ideas move. So by reasoning from the available data we might conclude either that Jesus did or that he did not say the things attributed to him, because one or another conclusion seemed to follow from the evidence.

There is another method which we might take which promises a more direct and speedy result. There are people whom we know so well that we can tell by instinct just what they would say on a certain subject. We have lived with them so long, we have become so familiar with their ways of thinking, that we do not need any one to tell us whether this or that is in keeping with their character. There are people who feel that they know Jesus in this way. If they find something attributed to him which contradicts the spirit of his teaching, they say, "No, he could not have said this. It is more reasonable to believe that his disciples misunderstood him, or that some scribe failed to transcribe the manuscript correctly." We might follow their example and make our own insight the final judge of the authenticity of the passage in dispute.

One other possible method is open to us, though here there are only a few sayings of Jesus to which it would seem to apply. Suppose the word whose authenticity we are trying to determine refers to some future experience which requires personal co-operation on our part. In the Gospel of Matthew, Jesus is reported to have said, "Where two or three are gathered together in my name there am I in the midst of them."[6] That is a strange saying. It is hard for us to see how Jesus, who died so many years ago, can be with us now. But that fact is not in itself conclusive.

[6] Matt. 18:20.

We believe that Jesus saw farther than we, for often in the past we have found him right when we thought him wrong. We will, therefore, not prejudge the case adversely, but will put the matter to the test which Jesus himself applied, the test of experiment. We will yield our spirit completely to the leading of his Spirit and see what happens. If in fact we become conscious of his presence with us to-day, it will make it easier to believe that the word which anticipates that presence was really spoken by him.

Now it is not difficult to show that, while all four of these methods may be used in determining the question which of Jesus' words are authentic, not all are equally legitimate or equally efficacious. In dealing with questions of fact in the narrow sense, like the date of an event or the correctness of a report, evidence of the first two kinds is ordinarily determining. We rely upon the testimony of those who know or reason by inference to what is probable. Intuition and experiment may serve as useful checks, but by themselves they can rarely bring the certainty we seek. But there are other questions where it is they that must speak the deciding word. When the matter to be determined is not what was said but the significance of the saying, we are apt to rely either upon our intuitive response to its truth or beauty or upon the confirmation which is brought to us by experiment. And where it is not a question of the word spoken but of the person who speaks, the importance to be attributed to intuition becomes even greater.

4. How the Nature of the Belief to Be Tested Determines the Method to Be Used

How the Scientist's Use of the Four Ways Differs from That of the Religious Man

In deciding what weight to give to each of the four ways we follow in our quest of certainty, therefore, we must first be clear which is most appropriate for the issue which we wish to decide. Where we are studying physical phenomena like gravitation or electricity, the mathematical methods of exact science are appropriate; where personality is the subject of our inquiry other methods are essential. Here the feelings and the will, as well as the mind, have their contribution to make. In our study of nature the personal equation must be eliminated so far as it is possible to do so. In our study of persons it has an indispensable contribution to make.

This reminder is the more necessary in view of the tendency, more than once referred to, to limit trustworthy knowledge to judgments which are reached through the methods of the exact sciences. That method is determined by its subject matter, namely, the uniformities of nature which make prediction possible. In studying a subject of this kind the restrictions which science imposes upon itself are not only legitimate but inevitable. But when we are dealing with realities like personality or with ideals like beauty or goodness other methods are in place. Here judgments of value, far from being disturbing factors, become the instruments through which alone trustworthy knowledge can be had.

We may illustrate this difference of aim in connection with each one of the four ways of testing belief. All four of them are used by scientists as well as by ordinary people, but in ways that are appropriate to their special aim.

Thus the scientist uses the method of intuition. Like all independent thinkers, he relies in the last analysis upon the conviction of truth which comes to him through his own immediate insight. But in his use of intuition he concentrates his attention upon those aspects of the subject in which the personal equation is least in evidence. Where his personal likes or dislikes are involved, he distrusts his conclusions and claims certainty only for those findings on which the senses can give a trustworthy report.

In like manner he uses the method of authority, but the only authority that he recognizes is that of the experts who have studied the subject before him. He takes their consensus of opinion as the basis of his own hypothesis and if he does not himself repeat their experiments it is only because he thinks it needless to do over again what men in whose accuracy and impartiality he has confidence have already done.

Again, he uses the method of reasoning. He compares all possible alternatives in order to clear his hypothesis of ambiguity and he refuses to consider any hypothesis as proved while any single fact remains in his universe with which it appears to be inconsistent. Probability is not enough. He will be satisfied with nothing less than complete demonstration.

But it is in the use of experiment that the excellencies and the limitations of the scientific method most clearly appear. No feature of modern scientific procedure is more remarkable than the ingenuity which it has employed in devising methods by which alternative possibilities can be isolated and their relevancy or irrelevancy to the situation under investigation can be determined. But the nature of the proof that is sought limits the experiments used to those which produce results which are capable of mathematical tests. For the great insights which have come to man in his best moments—to a Socrates in his prison, to a Jesus in the Garden—no system of measurement has yet been devised.

Within the limits thus set science is able to secure for us a very high degree of certainty. It can tell us when the sun will rise and how fast it will move, when to expect an eclipse and how it has been brought about, what combinations of elements make up specific substances and how they can be modified by heat or strain. It can tell us what drugs produce healing effects and how different people will react to them under prescribed conditions. It can tell us how the condition of the nervous system affects our mental states and which brain centres control perception, and which, action. The catalog of all the different things it can tell us would fill many volumes, and within the range which it has set itself its answers are trustworthy. When we do what the scientists tell us to do within the fields where their conclusions agree, the results which they promise follow. It does not occur to us for a moment to question that they will follow. Indeed the sequence has become so familiar to us that we often forget the complicated process by which man's mastery of nature has been brought about.

But there are other matters, and these no less important, to which this way of approach is not applicable. When we are dealing not with facts or with sequences of facts but with the meanings they suggest and the purposes they serve, other methods are essential. What these methods are we may learn by watching the procedure of those to whom the world has accorded the first place in the field of letters or of art.

Thus in his use of authority the poet or the artist will give chief weight to those witnesses whose experience has been characterized by the most vivid sense of beauty or of proportion, in other words to those aspects of reality in which judgments of value play the largest part.

So in his use of intuition, instead of discounting the significance of his personal satisfaction as expressed in his response to ideals of nobility or of beauty, the artist will make this satisfaction central among the grounds of his faith. But he will guard against the danger of subjectivity by subordinating his transient mood to his permanent attitude, and checking his own experience by comparing it with that of the artists who have found satisfaction in beauty before him.

Reasoning, too, will have its place in his test of certainty. And by reasoning he will mean what the scientist means by that term—the attempt to reach a conclusion which is consistent with all other knowledge. Indeed it is just because he respects the principle of consistency so highly that he is not willing to accept the scientist's account of the world as adequate. How can any view which, for however laudable a motive, excludes from consideration one great segment of the many-sided realm of reality claim to give a view of the world which is consistent with the facts.[7] Even if the artist cannot see how the values in life, as he sees it, can be reconciled with the facts of error or pain or death, he is not willing on that account to discredit these values. Somehow they must find their place in the total picture of reality and, even if he cannot as yet work out the reconciliation in detail, he will hold to his faith that a reconciliation will some day be possible. In the meantime he is grateful for all the light which science can shed upon the matters that fall within its own immediate province and, in so far as its conclusions have been established, will take them up into his own synthesis.

[7] *Cf.* Whitehead, A. N., *The Function of Reason* (Princeton, 1929), p. 12.

"Many a scientist has patiently designed experiments for the *purpose* of substantiating his belief that animal operations are motivated by no purpose. He has perhaps spent his spare time in writing articles to prove that human beings are as other animals so that 'purpose' is a category irrelevant for the explanation of their bodily activities, his own activities included. Scientists animated by the purpose of proving that they are purposeless constitute an interesting subject for study."

But it is in experiment that the likeness and the unlikeness of the two procedures most clearly appear. Like the scientist, the artist makes large use of experiment, but it is experiment of a different kind. The experiments of the exact sciences are concerned with parts, or aspects, of reality and achieve their end in the measure that, by analysis, they segregate the parts to be investigated from others which, in life, are intimately associated with them. The experiments of art, on the other hand, are concerned with the effects produced upon us by the world as a whole, or by the lesser wholes of which it is composed—mountains and sea and trees and flowers and men and women. The aim of the artist is to exhibit the true relation between these different wholes, as that relation is illuminated by comprehensive ideals, like beauty, or honor, or goodness, and life as it is actually lived by men and women is the laboratory in which the artist verifies by experiment the correctness of his original intuition of the ideal.

These considerations we must bear in mind in our approach to the object of religious certainty, which is God. God is not an isolated fact which can be separated from its environment and demonstrated, as we can demonstrate the weight of a man or the date of an eclipse. God is the ultimate reality in the universe, the moving spirit in all nature and in all history, and everything that happens, whether in us or apart from us, may contribute to our understanding of his nature and will. To know God in the sense in which religion understands knowledge is not sim-

ply to apprehend him with the mind. It is to reverence and to obey him. In validating a belief so comprehensive we should not expect to secure the desired
result by any purely intellectual process. Rather
should we hope to find our confidence justified by the
converging evidence of all possible methods of approach.

Is Revelation a Fifth Way?

But I am sure that long before this some of my
readers will have been saying to themselves, Why
limit the paths to be followed in our quest of certainty to four? Surely there is a fifth way open to
us, the most direct and dependable of all, namely, the
broad highway of divine revelation. All the methods
we have been studying are no doubt good methods as
far as they go. But they are human methods. And
where the final responsibility rests with man there
is always the possibility of mistake. The certainty of
which we are in search in religion, on the other hand,
is divine certainty. How can we find God unless he
himself comes to meet us; and when he speaks how
can there be any doubt as to what he says?

There is the best of authority for such a reminder.
Belief in a definite and easily accessible revelation has
been one of the oldest and most persistent of human
beliefs. The Catholic finds such a revelation in the
church, the Protestant in the Bible, the mystic in the
immediate witness of God's Spirit to the spirit of
man. Bible and church bring God's message in explicit terms of universal validity. The mystic revela-

tion on the other hand is private and personal. Yet in each case the one to whom the revelation comes is sure that it is God with whom he has to do, and in each case the communication received has an authentic quality which seems to the recipient to preclude the possibility of mistake.

Waiving for a moment the question whether even divine revelation can preclude the possibility of mistake in man's understanding of it, it is sufficient here to point out that God's revelation when it comes will be found not outside the four ways already distinguished but inside. The Catholic, as we have seen, hears God speaking to him through the church, the Protestant through the Bible. But these are the two outstanding examples of the method of authority. The mystic, for his part, tells us that he needs no external authority, for he has heard God's Spirit speaking directly to his own spirit. But the witness of the Spirit is only the religious man's way of describing what the psychologist calls intuition. Even reason, the way of all ways that is most often set over against revelation as man's way in contrast to God's, is recognized by theologians of all schools as a form, even though a lower form, of revelation.[8]

Revelation then is not to be thought of as a fifth

[8] It is easy to see why religious people should associate divine revelation most directly with the methods of intuition and of authority. They operate more quickly than the methods of reasoning and of experiment and in a more direct and personal way. Yet if, as we believe, God is the God of the whole world, no road that leads to him can be unimportant and the slower ways, just because they require the co-operation of all parts of our nature—mind and will, as well as feeling—may lead to a certainty all the more satisfying.

way of reaching certainty, to be added to the other four ways as supplying us with additional material. Rather is it our way of expressing our conviction that in each of the four ways God is speaking to us and that no account of his ways of revealing himself can be complete which does not take them all in. God does speak to us through authority in the testimony of his Bible and of his church. He does speak to us through his Spirit in the intuitions of our best moments. But it is one thing to recognize the existence of a real God, who is really revealing himself to us, and another to contrast that revelation not only with some of our subjective imaginings about him but with every conceivable process through which we men acquire knowledge. This is easy to do in words, difficult to do in fact. And while the motive is a natural and, in many respects, a laudable one, namely, to lift us above the uncertainties of our human apprehension and plant our feet upon the firm rock of divine truth, it will be found that the short cut does not lead to the goal as speedily as we thought.[9] On the contrary, we shall discover that the pathway of revelation will lead us before we are through into each

[9] Let us take the case where the contrast between revelation and our other ways of knowing appears in its most distinct and characteristic form, namely, belief in miracle. It will be found that even here all four ways of knowing must contribute to our certainty. The purpose of miracle, we are told, is to lift us above the uncertainties of reason and ground our faith upon an unshakable foundation. But before the miracle can convince us we must be convinced of the miracle, and here all four ways of knowing must be called into play. First we must prove that the alleged miraculous event really happened; and for this proof we have to rely either upon our own direct experience or upon the testimony of others—in other words, upon intuition or authority. And when

one of the other four paths which are now to be the
subject of our study: the path of authority, the path
of intuition, the path of reasoning, and the path of
experiment, and that it is only when we have traversed the territory covered by them all that we shall
arrive at last at our goal.

we have proved that it really happened as reported we must still
be able to show that it was really a miracle and not simply a
strange fact that we have not been able to explain. Here again we
must make use of the same methods that other men would use in
a similar case, namely, reasoning and experiment. We compare
the alleged miracle with other known events and conclude that it
must have had a cause that was different in kind, and we are confirmed in the correctness of this judgment by the fact that all
later experiment has been unable to reproduce it.

CHAPTER III

The Way of Authority: or What Others Can Tell Us About God

1. What Is Meant by Authority.

Two Meanings of Authority—Why External Authority Is Necessary—Authority as a Form of Revelation —Possible Attitudes Toward Inherited Belief.

2. Bible and Church as Forms of Authority.

The Church as Authority—The Bible as Authority— The Modern Revolt Against Authority.

3. What Authority Can Do For Us.

How Science Uses Authority—An Analogy in the Religious Sphere—The Contribution of Authority to Our Thought of God—Bible and Church as Sources of Christian Belief—The Contribution of Authority to Our Appreciation of God.

4. The Sense in Which Jesus Is Authority to His Disciples.

Jesus as a Teacher and as a Symbol—In What Sense Jesus Is Authority to the Christian.

Authority in its widest sense means the right to control, whether that right be exercised by others or by our own ideals. In the more restricted sense of a standard imposed from without it is the easiest and it is still the most generally used of the pathways to certainty. In Christianity its most familiar forms are the Bible and the Church. In our day we find a widespread revolt against authority in all forms, due in large part to the unjustified claims which have been made on its behalf. Catholics assert for the Church, and Protestants have often asserted for the Bible, an infallible authority which makes its witness final in all matters on which it speaks. But this claim, even if it could be established, is found to need revision at two points. For one thing it is not always possible to determine just when Bible and Church have spoken in this infallible way. For another, when this has been determined, it is often impossible to secure agreement as to what the message means. The way out of the difficulty is not to reject authority as a pathway to certainty but to define more clearly just what authority is fitted to do for us. Authority gives us a working basis by which to live during the period when we are too immature to test our beliefs for ourselves. When maturity comes it brings before us in concise and manageable form what belief in God has meant in the lives of our predecessors, so that when we test our own beliefs we may be furnished with all the help which the past can give us.

1. What Is Meant by Authority

Two Meanings of Authority

The easiest of the four ways of reaching certainty is the way of authority and it is still the way most commonly used in our day. With this therefore we begin.

The word authority is used in two senses. In the most general sense it is used to describe the quality of any conviction which impresses itself upon us with irresistible force, whether the constraint come to us from without or from within. This is the sense in which Martineau uses it in his book, *The Seat of Authority in Religion.*[1] By authority, he tells us, we mean anything that has the right to control, whether that right is exercised by another or by one part of ourselves over other parts. Thus conscience can rightly be called authoritative, since it speaks to us with the categorical imperative, even though no one hears but ourselves. The distinguishing mark of authority is its irresistible character. On the basis of this broader definition, intuition would be a form of authority.

Usually, however, the word is taken in a more restricted sense. By authority we mean some standard external to ourselves which determines for us what we shall think or what we shall do. Law is an authority

[1] London, 1890.

83

in this sense, whether it be religious or secular, and the government which imposes law.

In this chapter we shall use the word authority in the narrower sense. We shall mean by it the sum of the convictions which we take over from others before we have had the opportunity to test them ourselves.

Why External Authority Is Necessary

Our study of the psychology of belief has shown us that this is the way in which we first acquire all our religious beliefs. We believe in a righteous, loving God because we live in a world where people already believe in such a God. We believe in such a God because our parents believed in him, or our teachers, or the friends we know best and trust most. Belief in God is a part of our inheritance from the past which it does not occur to us to question, at least at first. There are many people who never question it at all.

There is nothing in this attitude to be ashamed of. So far as it goes it is entirely defensible. If it were not for social tradition there would be no progress in knowledge. What one generation learns it transmits to its successors as the point of departure for further experiment. No scientist can test everything, even in his own field. Life would not be long enough for this. Much must be taken over on the authority of experts who have gone before. Why should we expect it to be otherwise in religion?

It is not simply convenient to believe in God because others have done so; to men of a certain temperament it seems reasonable to do so. The fact that through so many ages men have believed in God; that the company of believers has included thinkers like Augustine, statesmen like Cromwell, and saints like Francis; the further fact that the belief has continued in spite of all our advance in knowledge and of all the changes in our social environment, creates a presumption in favor of the truth of the belief which commends it to our respectful consideration.

Thus there are logical as well as psychological reasons for accepting authority. When Chief Justice Taney was once asked how it happened that he, a man of independent judgment and trained intellect, could accept the teaching of the Roman Catholic Church, which at so many points seemed to contradict reason, he is reported to have answered that his training as a lawyer had taught him the value of expert knowledge. "When I want to know about law," he said, "I go to a lawyer; when I want to know about religion, I go to the Church."

Not only is the method of authority the most convenient of the methods; it is also the most universal. The best way to assure oneself of this is to watch what happens to those who try to dispense with it altogether. Sooner or later we shall find them setting up a new authority to take the place of the old and paying to it, consciously or unconsciously—quite as often unconsciously as consciously—all the reverence and submission which they once paid to the old. One bids good-bye to the Bible only to set up a new mentor in psycho-analysis or behaviorist psychology and the place vacated by Isaiah or St. Paul is taken by Professor Freud or Professor Watson.

The way of authority, I repeat, is an ancient and a well-worn way. We begin to tread it from the first moment of our conscious life and, however long we may live, we never come to the place where we can dispense with it. All of us take over a mass of beliefs from the social environment in which we live and test only that part of it which is challenged or which bears directly upon some personal interest of urgent importance. When the testing takes place it does not necessarily mean that we replace the method of authority by another; it may mean simply that we use other methods to clarify our understanding of what the old authority teaches, or that we substitute a new authority for the old.

Authority as a Form of Revelation

It is not strange, in view of the large place which authority plays in daily life, that many people should regard it as the final test of right belief in religion, for it seems to give us what we most need to lift us above our human uncertainties—a definite word of God on which we can rest with confidence. For many religious people, therefore, revelation and authority become synonyms. To believe in a self-revealing God means to them to surrender individual initiative and to accept without question a decision made by another.

There are times in human life when it is necessary
to do this. While we are children and have not yet
learned to think for ourselves; when we are under
such pressure of instant duty that there is no time to
think; when we are dealing with questions which
transcend our human powers and on which we possess no data on which intelligent decisions can be
based; and again in those rarer moments when, after
long-continued weighing of the evidence, the scales
seem equally balanced and we find ourselves unable
to come to a conclusion: at these times we instinctive-
ly turn to the accumulated wisdom of the past and
let authority decide for us.

But this temporary use of authority, legitimate
and even necessary though it be, is quite a different
thing from making authority the sole, or even the
final, form of divine revelation. To understand the
difficulties which arise when we try to do this we must
consider the different forms in which authority meets
us.

Possible Attitudes Toward Inherited Belief

The beliefs of the past have come down to us as
convictions tested by generations of personal experience and also as doctrines or creeds which state the
content of these convictions in definite propositions.
Often, but not always, these two forms coincide. Our
creeds express convictions of permanent validity, but
they do so ordinarily in forms which reflect the conditions of the time in which they were formulated, its
prevailing philosophy, its inadequate science. It is

necessary to distinguish the truth affirmed from its transient setting.

Many religious people, perhaps the majority, use the inheritance of the past in an uncritical way. They accept the creeds and catechisms at their face value and do not question their trustworthiness at any point. Indeed, it would seem to them irreligious to do so. Such an unquestioning acceptance of traditional views is often consistent with a sincere and effective religious life. The energy which might have gone into intellectual inquiry is directed to practical living, and those who would be hard put to it to give a reason for their faith in words, give it most effectively in their lives.[2]

---

[2] Speaking of the reasons which led to his conversion to Roman Catholicism, Father Vernon Johnson has this to say of the impression produced on him by studying the life of St. Thérèse, of Lisieux:

"She [St. Thérèse] had, indeed, the capacity to cling by Faith in the darkest moments and to believe things beyond her reason; but she had all this in a unique degree because, behind and beneath it all, was a supernatural certainty in those Divine truths which she knew had been revealed and which she never for one moment doubted or questioned. These truths she did not question; not because her reason led her to believe in them, but because they were taught by an authority outside her which she knew to possess a divinely given authority which could never err or contradict itself in matters of faith. And it was because she was resting on this foundation that, free from endless controversies, her soul was able to grow and develop in such a marvellous way.

"I had always regarded such certainty in matters of faith as something impossible in this world and not even to be desired; because it could only be achieved at the expense of character and intellect, and by crippling all sincerity and growth. I held that thinking things out for oneself was the condition of character.

"And yet, here I was faced with the fact that it was precisely this certainty coming to St. Thérèse from an objective authority outside her which had produced the most intelligently saintly life I had known."—(*One Lord, One Faith.* Quoted by Frederick Lynch, in *American Church Monthly*, June, 1930.)

Nevertheless, such an unthinking faith has its dangers. At any moment a doubt may arise which cannot be summarily dealt with. Science, the most pervasive of all the influences of our modern world, may make a breach in the wall of dogma which has hitherto been identified with absolute truth, and this may mean the destruction not only of the wall but also of the truth which it was meant to protect. A leading scientist, who had lent his name to a prosecution for heresy, was once asked how it happened that a professor of geology in a great modern university could act as he did toward an eminent scholar in a sister field. "It is perfectly simple," he is reported to have answered. "In my brain I have two compartments, separated by a watertight wall. In one I keep my science, in the other my religion. If a breach should be made and my science should get over into my religion, good-bye to my religion."

But there is another conception of authority which is not exposed to this danger. We may think of it not as a substitute for first-hand experience, but as a convenient summary of the convictions to which men have thus far been brought by the experience of the past. We may think of Bible and church, not as giving us a set of abstract propositions about God which we are to take just as we find them, but as the record of what men have learned about God and what effect the resulting belief has had on their lives. When we hear Jesus speaking of the Father in heaven, or Paul proclaiming himself an ambassador of Christ, we may treat what they say just as we would treat the words of a friend who told us about the properties of radium or invited us to test a new motor to see whether it was able to do what its maker promised. Their words would not be a reason for dispensing with investigation, but rather a ground for thinking such investigation worth while.

There are two points at which our personal responsibility with reference to authority cannot be evaded. We are responsible in the first place, for the choice of the right authority. We are responsible, in the second place, for the right use of the authority we have chosen.

We may illustrate this double responsibility in connection with the two most important forms in which the claim to final authority meets us in Christianity, the church and the Bible.

2. BIBLE AND CHURCH AS EXAMPLES OF AUTHORITY

The Church as Authority

The oldest and the most widely recognized of all the forms of external authority is the church. It antedates the Bible and, in its Roman form at least, claims to interpret it. Its witness is continuous, easily accessible, and, for multitudes of religious people, decisive.

Protestants and Catholics agree that the church is a divine institution, having for its function the preaching of the Gospel, the celebration of divine worship, and the nurture of its members in the Christian life. Both alike have formulated their beliefs in creeds and crystallized their worship in ritual. Both alike set apart chosen ministers to interpret the creeds and to be leaders in worship. To the unthinking Christian, whether he be Protestant or Catholic, the authority of the church is not something definitely located in some particular part of this many-sided institution. It is the cumulative effect of the institution as a whole.

To the more thoughtful Christian, however, the authority of the church is something more specific and precise. It is found in its character as a divine institution, commissioned by God to reveal his will in definite and recognizable ways, and for this purpose furnished with the agencies which are necessary for its accomplishment. These agencies are the Bible, the creeds, the sacraments, and the ministry.

Catholics and Protestants differ radically in the importance which they attribute to these agencies and the way in which they conceive their function to be exercised. The Roman Catholic regards Bible, creed, and sacraments as authoritative, but only when interpreted by a continuing tradition of which the priest and, in the last analysis, the Pope, is the spokesman. The Protestant makes the Bible the final authority, but only as interpreted to the living church—in this case the whole body of the faithful— by the Holy Spirit. The content of this interpretation is preserved in the creeds and mediated in symbolic form through the sacraments. Apart from the living response of the individual through faith, the revelation (though authoritative) remains ineffective.

For those who desire an external authority which can relieve them of the responsibility of final decision, the position of the Roman Church seems to possess manifest advantages. That church offers itself as a present guide, able to give definite answers to the questions which are put to it and furnished with the necessary credentials to guarantee the trustworthiness of its answers. And for many a troubled spirit it has in fact furnished the certainty of which they were in search. Newman has described in classical language the sense of relief which came to him when he accepted this authority. Speaking of his own submission to Rome, after years of weary searching, he says, in his *Apologia:* "It was like coming into port after a rough sea."[3]

But the more closely we look into the security which Rome offers us, the more we perceive limitations which give us pause. Apart from the question of the credentials which validate its witness, it appears on investigation that that witness is both less frequent and less definite than we could wish. There are many questions on which we would like light on which the church has not spoken; others on which it has spoken, but not infallibly; still others on which it has spoken infallibly, but in ways which make possible different interpretations. For practical purposes the devout Catholic may find the solution of his difficulties in the disciplinary power of the church, which

[3] *Apologia pro vita sua* (London, 1890), p. 238.

has the right to exact obedience even in matters where infallibility is not involved. But for the inquiring spirit who seeks truth in the inward parts, the possibilities of question are almost unlimited. That Rome has spoken one may know, but what the utterance means may remain as mysterious as the word of the Sybil. Even the theologians, whose business it is to deal with meanings, are not agreed.

The Bible as Authority

From this confusion the Reformers found relief by substituting the Bible for the church. Here they were confident was an authority at once more accessible and less ambiguous. And so to many it proved. In God's word, spoken through the Bible, they found a message clear-cut, satisfying, fitted to their deepest need. Within this single volume God had compressed in a form intelligible to the simplest believer all that was necessary to be known, believed, and practised for salvation.[4]

The case of Luther is typical of what the Bible has done for many a distressed spirit. Luther was facing in his own life the sense of personal failure which is so familiar a human experience. The more he tried to secure inward satisfaction by outward conformity, the more he became conscious of the gap between ideal and attainment. One day a copy of the New Testament came into his hands and he read of

[4] *Cf. Westminster Confession,* chap. I, 1: "which maketh the Holy Scripture to be most necessary, those other ways of God's revealing his will unto his people being now ceased."

a man who through faith in Jesus Christ had found what he had sought in vain. The scales fell from his eyes and he recognized in the book that had brought him this insight God's word addressed to him.

What the Bible did for Luther it has done for many another who has come to it for a like purpose and used it in the same way. But for this it must be used as Luther used it, as a book of personal religion bringing personal answers to the deepest questions of the soul. When, as soon happened, Protestants began to extend the authority of the Bible to cover all matters of which it treats they became involved in all but insuperable difficulties. They found passages which seemed to contradict one another, and this not only in relatively unimportant points of science or of history but in matters of theology and of ethics as well.

Thus on the alleged authority of the Bible rival systems of doctrine were erected and incorporated in creeds to which assent was demanded as the condition of church membership, or at least of ministerial standing. When this happened the authority of the Bible was in fact superseded by the authority of the church or, to speak more exactly, of the churches.

The Modern Revolt Against Authority

These differences, present almost from the first in Protestantism, have been greatly accentuated by modern critical study. In the crucible of this study the unity which the older theory assumed disappears.

In place of a unique revelation, consistent in all its parts, we find in the Bible the story of a progressive training, in which men of very different types and of very different degrees of intellectual and moral maturity have been gradually enlightened as to the nature and purposes of God. So the church, instead of an infallible institution which preserves its form unchanged from generation to generation, proves in fact to reflect in its teaching all the variations of contemporary thought and to illustrate in the course of its nineteen centuries of history each of the most important forms of political organization.

Walter Lippmann, in the book already referred to, has pictured in vivid language the effects which have followed from the loss of the old authorities:

"By the dissolution of their ancestral ways men have been deprived of their sense of certainty as to why they were born, why they must work, whom they must love, what they must honor, where they may turn in sorrow and defeat. They have left to them the ancient codes and the modern criticism of these codes, guesses, intuitions, inconclusive experiments, possibilities, probabilities, hypotheses. Below the level of reason, they may have unconscious prejudice, they may speak with a loud cocksureness, they may act with fanaticism. But there is gone that ineffable certainty which once made God and His Plan seem as real as the lamppost."[5]

Mr. Lippmann does not indeed affirm that modern men have ceased to believe in God. He asserts that "they no longer believe in him simply and literally," as they believe, for example, in the existence of their

[5] *Op. cit.*, p. 21.

neighbors whom they can see and hear and touch.[6]

It may be questioned whether even in the palmiest days of orthodoxy thoughtful men believed in God quite so simply and naïvely as Mr. Lippmann seems to think. In all the churches there existed, side by side with a crude and literal faith, a way of thinking about God which conceived of Him in symbolic terms, suggestive rather than descriptive, much as modern physics uses symbols to suggest its conception of mysterious natural forces like electricity. The most authoritative Christian teachers were well aware that when they spoke of God as personal or as good, when they described him as exercising foresight or having judgment, they were using terms derived from our finite experience to suggest a reality which transcended that experience in ways incapable of exact definition. Yet they felt justified in doing so because such terms, like the corresponding symbols of science, helped to make more intelligible phenomena in their own lives and in the lives of others of which they had first-hand knowledge.

This way of conceiving of God is still open to the modern thinker. The fact remains that, with the loss of the old definiteness, something has dropped out which makes faith more difficult for many of our contemporaries, and for some makes it impossible. It is not that modern men are not willing to accept authority. That is occasionally true, but not of the majority of men. It is that they *cannot* accept it even if they would. They do "not wantonly reject belief, as

[6] *Ibid.*

so many churchmen assert." Their "predicament is much more serious. With the best will in the world" they find themselves "not quite believing."[7]

3. WHAT AUTHORITY CAN DO FOR US

How Science Uses Authority

When we analyze the difficulties which the modern man feels when dealing with authority we find that they reduce to two. Either he objects to authority on principle, because it attempts to relieve him of the responsibility which is rightfully his, or he rejects it on practical grounds, because it promises a service which it is unable to perform.

And it must be admitted that as against the conception of authority to which we have given most of our attention both of these objections have great force. The chief reason why many people are urged to accept authority in the clear-cut and definite form in which it meets us in church and in Bible is that it may relieve them of the responsibility for ultimate decision; yet when they attempt to use it in this way they find that it does not in fact succeed in doing so. Within the territory in which authority operates they find that there are still momentous decisions to be made, and neither Bible nor church can relieve them of the responsibility of making them.

We have seen, however, that there is another conception of authority which is familiar to our modern world against which these objections do not apply. It

[7] *Op. cit.*, p. 56.

is the authority of the expert whom we trust in matters within the sphere of his competence, not because we ourselves have verified his conclusions or indeed ever expect wholly to do so, but because we believe that they are capable of verification and that, if we were to qualify ourselves for the test as he has done, we should find our conclusions tallying with his. We trust him, in other words, because he brings us the result of tests which we might, if we would, perform for ourselves.

This does not mean that we accept everything the expert tells us or follow him in all the arguments with which he supports his conclusions. He would himself be the last to expect such unquestioning loyalty. He knows that in every field of research there is a wide range of debatable territory and that at many points those who have studied most are far from agreement. But in every science there is a central core of agreement which represents the consensus of the best opinion up to date and we look to the expert to tell us what this consensus is and how it bears upon the practical questions which we have to decide. We may not follow the expert in all his arguments, but by acting upon the principles he recommends we contribute our part to the verification of his conclusions.

This is the real ground for the layman's confidence in modern science. When he reads the works of its latest expositors, even such masters of English as Whitehead and Eddington, he may find himself at times hopelessly confused. What between relativity and the quantum theory he feels the solid ground shifting under his feet and all his familiar landmarks crumbling. But when he forgets the theories of the scientists and acts on that part of their conclusions which bears directly upon his daily life he finds that their advice is to be trusted. The trains they build carry him to his destination. The lamps they furnish give him the light he needs. The electricity they harness carries his messages. The remedies they provide heal his diseases. This practical verification, in which not the expert simply, but the layman, is concerned, is the real reason why we attribute to science, within the sphere which is properly its own, a very real authority.

An Analogy in the Religious Sphere

A similar attitude is possible to the religious authorities of which we have been speaking. We may trust Bible and church, not because we can understand all that they tell us, not even because all their statements agree at all points with one another, but because when we act upon what they tell us in the central practical matters on which they are agreed we find that the results we have a right to expect follow. Our experience confirms the experience of our predecessors and contributes its share to the body of evidence which we pass on to the generations that follow us.[8]

[8] This is the real meaning of that much misunderstood doctrine of Protestantism, the universal priesthood of believers. This does not mean that all Christians are equally competent to speak on all matters of religion or that there is no place for the expert to tell us what we ought to believe or to do, but it does mean that we

This is in fact the way in which religious people have always used authority, so far as they have really used it and not simply made it an excuse for dispensing with any attempt to secure that vivid consciousness of the reality of God which it is the function of authority to make possible. Catholics have not concerned themselves with everything the church has said, but only with those aspects of the church's teaching which bear directly upon their personal lives. Protestants have not treated everything in the Bible as of equal importance. Each of them has had his own little Bible within the Bible, which consists of the central passages to which he has gone back from day to day because they met some deep spiritual need within himself or gave him guidance as to the right course of action when he faced alternative choices. Each of them has been constantly reinterpreting these passages in the light of his own growing experience and deepening insight; and the devotional literature of the church is the result of this progressive reinterpretation.

But the real situation has been obscured by the fact that there has often been a discrepancy between theory and practice. Protestants have continued to speak of the Bible as if its authority were of one kind, while at the same time they have used it as if its authority were of another kind. The same has been

cannot take his word about God as final for us until we have put it to the test of our own life. It means that to the final proof that God is really what the great masters of religion have told us he is, the experience of even the least of his children has its contribution to make.

true, though to a lesser degree, of the attitude of
many Catholics toward the church. The time has
come when the true function of authority in religion
needs to be reconceived, so that we may conscientious-
ly avail ourselves of the help it is fitted to give without sacrificing our intellectual honesty. We need to
realize that it is not necessary for us to surrender the
conviction that God is speaking to us in Bible and in
church because we have discovered that the process
through which his revelation reaches us is a longer
and more complicated one than our fathers supposed
and that, if it is to do for us what it is fitted to do,
we must make use of the methods of progressive verification and redefinition through which all our progress in knowledge comes.

The Contribution of Authority to Our Thought of God

With so much of preface let us turn back to the
authorities which religious men have recognized in
the past and see how far, as thus reconceived, they
are open to the criticisms which many of our contemporaries bring against them. These criticisms, we
have seen, are two: either that they attempt to relieve us of the responsibility which is rightfully ours,
or that, granting their right to do this, they promise
us a service which in fact they are unable to perform.
It is clear that the first objection can fairly be
brought only against an authority that promises an
infallible certainty which needs no later verification
or revision. In fact, as we have seen, when tested by

their actual operation, neither church nor Bible has
functioned in this way. Each has made heavy demand upon the initiative of those who have used its
authority. Indeed, it may prove that one of the reasons why so many of our contemporaries have abandoned the older authorities is not because they made
light demands upon the reason but because their demands were heavy. Authority for authority, Professor Watson and Professor Freud have proved
easier masters to follow than St. Paul or St. Augustine.

The real difficulty, I suspect, for most people is the
second rather than the first. It is not that authority
offers to do too much for us, but that it succeeds in
doing too little.

Recent interpreters of the modern mind, as we
have seen, contrast the clear-cut views about God
which were held by the men of an earlier generation
with the haziness and indefiniteness of much modern
thinking about the deity; and they find this indefiniteness accentuated rather than decreased by the results of modern critical study. That study shows us
not only the contrast between the naïve beliefs of
popular religion, which conceive of God as a kind of
glorified superman, sitting upon a throne above the
heavens and interfering in earth's affairs now and
again in arbitrary ways, and the views of those thinkers who emphasize the elements of mystery and tran-
scendence in our conception of the deity; it shows us
also that the great religious teachers have differed
radically in their conceptions of the nature of God

and of his relation to the world which he has made.

And if the function of authority were to give us a definite and final view of God which is never at any point to be revised, this would be a fatal objection. But if, on the contrary, the function of authority is not to relieve us of responsibility but to help us to discharge it effectively, the objection no longer holds. Then what we find is only what we should expect to find.

In dealing with a fact so many-sided, so elusive, yet so intimate and familiar as the fact of God, we cannot expect any single statement to include all that we need to know. All that we can rightfully ask of authority is that it shall tell us in the language that is appropriate to the time and the circumstances what the men who have made earnest with the fact of God before us believed that they had found and why they believed it.

Bible and Church as Sources of Christian Belief

The Bible does just this for us. It tells us how the Christian religion began and what faith in God meant to the men who received their impulse to the religious life from their fellowship with Jesus. It tells us what God meant to Jesus; what he took over from the great prophets and seers who had preceded him; what he contributed out of his own experience; how contact with his person added a new symbol to the older forms through which his predecessors had tried to make real to themselves the nature of God. It tells us how the old words, justice, wisdom, righteousness,

love, in which in religion after religion men have expressed their ideals of the divine, received new meaning from the story of his life and death and continuing influence. And it tells us not only what the early
Christians thought about God but what effect this
thought had upon their lives. It gives us the reasons
why they believed in him and why they continued to
believe in him in spite of the shocks of persecution
and apparent failure. As the oldest, the most direct,
and the most reliable source of our knowledge of the
historic Jesus, the founder of the Christian religion,
and of the creative period of the religion he founded,
the Bible will always remain the textbook of Christianity. No other book can take its place.

But the Bible alone is not enough. For without
the church the Bible would be only half understood.
The church tells us the story of what Jesus has meant
to all the generations which have come after him. In
its history we follow the course of the new religion as it
passes from one environment to another, winning to
itself new peoples, meeting the test of alien philosophies, developing new forms of organization, creat-
ing, and in turn being remoulded by, virile personalities. The various stages in this progressive development have been preserved for us in the successive
families of creeds and liturgies. Each represents a
phase of man's experience with God and as such has
something important to tell us. When I wish to
know what I have in common with the men of the first
four Christian centuries I cannot ignore the Apostles'
Creed or the Nicene Creed. When I would under-

stand my own spiritual lineage I turn back to the
records of the creative period of Protestantism, as it
is preserved in classical creeds like the Heidelberg
Catechism and the Westminster Confession. But
there are fresh insights which have been coming to
the church in these latter days and for these I must
rely on more recent utterances like the Social Creed
of the churches[10] and the messages of the great con-
ferences of Stockholm and of Lausanne.[11] These successive forms of the church's testimony are not mu-
tually exclusive, even though at points they do not
agree, so that when I take one I reject the others.
Each has something to contribute when it is used in
the right way and for the right purpose. The tradition of the church is not a series of academic formulæ, to be judged by the tests which are applied to
students in college or university. It is the life story
of a great spiritual movement, an imperishable part
of the priceless heritage of mankind.

In another volume[12] I have summed up the permanent convictions about God which have been the outcome of this age-long process and I need not repeat
in detail what was said there. To speak only of the
religion most familiar to us of the Western world,
Christians have thought of God as the ultimate reality, the mystery of mysteries, transcending man's

[10] *The Social Work of the Churches,* ed. F. Ernest Johnson
(New York, 1930), p. 123.
[11] *The Stockholm Conference on Life and Work, 1925,* ed. by G.
K. A. Bell (London, 1926), pp. 710–716.
   Faith and Order, Lausanne, 1927, ed. by H. N. Bate (New York,
1927), pp. 461–463.
[12] *Beliefs That Matter* (New York, 1928).

power to exhaust or to understand. They have thought of him as Creative Will, fashioning all things according to his wise and loving plan. They have thought of him as indwelling Spirit, immanent in nature and in man, the source of present insight in individuals and in society. They have thought of him as ideal personality, revealing his character and purpose to those who put their trust in him.

It would not be just to claim for Christianity a monopoly of these convictions concerning God. If, as Christians believe, God be the God of the whole world, we should expect to find evidence of his self-disclosure in other religions, and the more wide-spread and compelling these evidences prove to be, the stronger will be the Christian's conviction that in worshipping God, as Jesus revealed him, he is in touch with reality. Our reason for confining the present discussion to the particular view of God presented in Christianity is not that we minimize the importance of the other religions or undervalue the contribution which they may make to our understanding of God, but solely that we desire, in dealing with a subject so difficult, to concentrate on those aspects of it with which our readers are most familiar.

Thus neither Bible nor church alone can do for us what we need to have done. They are not rival authorities between which we must choose, so that if one chose the church one must reject the Bible, and *vice versa*. It is not a case of Bible *or* church but of Bible *and* church, each authoritative in its place for the uses which it is fitted to serve.

But if our test is to yield the desired result, we must do our part. Bible and church are not given to us ready-made to relieve us of effort on our part. They become to us really authoritative only when we use them as they were meant to be used, as opportunities to be embraced and possibilities to be tested.

The Contribution of Authority to Our Appreciation of God

There is a further contribution which authority is fitted to make to our sense of religious certainty which is of the first importance, although it is very generally overlooked. This is its power to train our religious emotions.

We have seen that the God of living religion stands in a dual relation, partly to the physical universe that we call nature, partly to the ideal world to which art and ethics belong. To understand all that he is and means we must use our minds and take account of whatever light the science of the time may shed upon the manner of his working; but we must also realize that he cannot be completely known even to the extent to which that knowledge is possible to us until we include among the sources of our knowledge our intuitions of beauty, of goodness, and of love.

This concern with the excellencies which faith discovers in God explains some recurrent aspects of the religious experience. It explains for one thing the emotional quality which is so permanent an element in this experience. For emotion attaches ordinarily to the qualitative aspect of life, the aspect which we distinguish as better or worse. To be religious is to feel awe in the presence of mystery. It is to find fascination in the contemplation of the creative. Religion brings to its devotees a thrill such as artists know when they contemplate beauty, a joy such as lovers feel when they lose themselves in the object of their devotion. Gratitude, penitence, adoration, ecstasy: these are familiar elements of vital religious experience.

Yet deeply as it stirs the emotions, religion is more than emotion. Common to all vital religion is the conviction that the experience it fosters brings man into touch with objective reality. Religion is not something which man invents or even discovers for himself. It is response to revelation. It is the discovery of a God who brings light as well as joy; indeed, who brings joy just because he brings light.[13]

We misconceive the function of authority then if we think of its contribution as merely, or even chiefly, intellectual. We learn from the witness of the past not only what our predecessors have thought about God but, what is more important, how they have felt about him and how they have acted toward him. They have a contribution to make not only to our understanding of God but to our appreciation of him.

We may illustrate this contribution in connection with both the forms of authority which we have been considering,—the Bible and the church. The Bible is in a very real sense a source-book of Christian doc-

[13] In his recent book, *An Emerging Christian Faith* (New York, 1930), Dr. Justin W. Nixon uses the term "givenness" to describe this aspect of the religious life.

trine. It tells us what Jesus thought about God, and what St. Paul thought, and what was thought by the writer of the Fourth Gospel. It gives us the thought forms in which they phrased their experience of deity, words like Creator, and Father, and King, that recur again and again in the later literature. But it reproduces for us also, and this is even more important, the mood of feeling which animated those who used them, the sense of awe which they felt when they realized the greatness and the majesty of God, the sense of gratitude that thrilled them when they realized that the Most High had visited them. When we read the Bible we feel the magnetism of vibrant personalities, seeking to share with those to whom they speak the reverence that has transformed their lives. No one can realize what the Bible has meant in the life of the church who does not appreciate that it has trained men in habits of feeling as well as schooled them in ways of thinking.

What is true of the Bible is true also of the church. We have spoken of the tradition of the church as contained in its creeds and in its ritual. But these are only one form, and not the most significant, of the church's authority. More impressive than anything the great churchmen have said has been the witness of their lives, the effect upon others of their consciousness of living in daily fellowship with the unseen, the contagious influence of their sense of mission.

This consciousness has been perpetuated not simply through the personal witness of men and women, but also through corporate acts which express common experiences and which interpret their reality to the senses as well as to the intellect. Christianity, if we take it in its main line of development, has been a sacramental religion, and in rites like baptism and the Lord's Supper has fostered a corporate consciousness which has bridged the gap of time and space and helped more effectively than argument alone could do to overcome man's innate tendency to provincialism. Coming under the spell of this corporate witness, we feel ourselves in the presence of a reality too august to be expressed in intellectual terms and we are encouraged to explore, each of us for himself, the possibilities of the life of prayer.

The Anglo-Catholics have felt the power of this corporate witness more strongly than any other group in our day. They have helped an age which has grown weary of criticism to rediscover the emotional appeal of authority. In the sense of reverence that is fostered by a great cathedral, perpetuating by means of statue and painted window memories of a simpler and more devout age; in the consciousness of fellowship with past generations—differing in race and language, yet made one through membership in a mystical body; in the solemn self-searching of an early morning communion, when, at the familiar words: "This is my body," the worshipper is thrilled by the sense of a presence not of this world, these modern Christians have experienced a renewal and enhancement of life which has made them sure that they are dealing directly with God.

Thus authority appeals to more than the mind.

It has a message to the emotions as well. Indeed it is through its appeal to the emotions, even more than through its challenge of the intellect, that it fulfills its most useful function. Thought is always restless, reaching out for that which is unattained, and it is its very nature so to do. Feeling grasps that which is immediately given and responds to it loyally. The greatest of all the gifts you can give a child is an object that naturally calls forth his loyalty. The greatest of all the examples you can set before a child is an example of devotion to an object which is in its essence worthy of loyalty.

4. The Sense in Which Jesus Is Authority to His Disciples

Jesus as a Teacher and as a Symbol

Such an object Christians have found in Jesus. From the first he has held the central place in Christianity. His words express convictions about God and his will that have remained normative in the life of his followers. What is more important, his life illustrates, as no merely spoken word could do, what righteousness and love may mean for daily living. Other teachers have said many, perhaps all, of the things which Jesus is reported to have said. No other teacher has impressed his followers as so completely embodying the truths which he taught. To Christians, therefore, the person of Jesus has an importance in their religion which is not held by the personality of the founder of any other religion. He is the leader whom they follow, the redeemer whom they trust, the symbol of everything that is most sacred and worthy in their ideal. And the authority of the church is exercised most significantly in this, that by introducing us to those who feel in this way about Jesus and by making us participant in their corporate acts it creates in us feelings which lead us to try Jesus for ourselves to see whether he does not indeed deserve our loyalty.

We look with concern, therefore, upon the attempt to discredit the authority of Jesus because the critics differ in their interpretation of his teaching or the reformers in their view of its bearing upon the moral problems of our day. Such an attitude misapprehends the true function of authority in the life of society. In dealing with great issues like belief in God or the nature of the ideal society complete intellectual agreement is not at any time attainable. Such agreement, could it be reached, would make impossible the progressive redefinition which is the condition of social progress. But just because the readjustment involved in the appropriation of new truth necessarily produces intellectual and moral tension, we need some common symbol expressive of the unities which persist in spite of change. The person of Jesus presents such an object of common loyalty which, admitting of different intellectual interpretations, makes fellowship possible in spite of difference and by so doing performs an indispensable social funtion.

This is indeed, as we have seen, the highest and

truest function of authority in any form, a function not intellectual primarily but moral. An authority, in the religious sense of that term, is a symbol that holds men by its emotional appeal while the process of criticism is being carried on and so prevents that process from becoming morally disintegrating.

So far, indeed, as the contemporary disposition to depreciate Jesus' authority represents a protest against the attempt to associate Jesus with a conception of authority which has been found untenable in connection with the Bible or the church we may welcome it. But when the conclusion is drawn that because we have sources of knowledge about physical nature, our own personality, or our common life in society, of which Jesus neither made nor could make use, he therefore loses his authority, we fall into an equally disastrous error. Of all the possessions of mankind none are more precious than the symbols that express our common loyalties. To multitudes in all lands and over many centuries the person of Jesus has been associated with their deepest convictions and their most sacred commitments, and through the possession of this common symbol they have won a sense of fellowship with one another. The man or the woman who attempts to sever this bond without gravest cause assumes a momentous responsibility. All the more because Jesus does not profess to instruct us in the learning of the schools; because his appeal is to the basic convictions which are central in our individual and social life; because he does not supersede but enhances and stimulates our personal responsibility, he may become in the truest sense an authority to the thoughtful modern men and women who will let him do for them what he is able to do.

In What Sense Jesus Is Authority to the Christian

Can we go farther than this and suggest specific ways in which Jesus may prove himself authority for the men and women of our day?

If we consult the experience of Christians in the past we shall find that there are three points in which the person of Jesus has been associated with their deepest and most fundamental convictions. They are points which touch in the most direct and intimate ways the central matters on which we saw at the outset that certainty is essential to us modern men. One concerns the goal of our living, the second the way in which that goal is to be attained, the third the resources available for the attainment of that goal.

Jesus has become to his disciples in the first place their clearest illustration of the kind of life they would like to see prevail everywhere in society. That life, as we have seen, is a life of sympathetic goodwill in which each co-operates with his neighbor for the common good. Christians have taken Jesus as their authority because he has helped them to understand better than any one they know what the world would be like if all the people in it were living a life of love.

Jesus further exemplifies to his disciples the kind of spirit that must prevail if the life of love is ever

to be realized in fact. There is only one way to realize
the ideal life, whether in oneself or in society, and
that is to begin the practice of loving as Jesus illustrated love in his attitude toward men. We must feel
toward our neighbors as our brothers. We must desire their good. We must be willing to do whatever
we see to be possible to make that good prevail,
even if we perish in the doing of it. It is for lack of
this spirit that some of the most promising programs
of social reform in our day fail of their effects. Men
may differ in many respects in their view of the way
in which the social goal is to be reached, but if this
spirit is present they will find ways of coming together. They may agree at almost every point in
their social philosophy. If the spirit of self-sacrifice
and of goodwill is lacking, nothing effective will be
done.

Once more Jesus symbolizes to his disciples the resources on which we must rely if the obstacles which
now impede the life of love in us and in others are
ever to be overcome. Jesus' life was flooded by the
inrush of a divine love which made him conscious of
fellowship with one who was able to supply his every
need. So he has become to his followers the symbol of
what God is like and the channel whereby the love of
God may find access to the spirits of men.

The disciples of Jesus have not arrived at these
convictions about him primarily by the way of intellectual analysis but by living under his influence as a
friend might live with his friend. They offer them to
us to use as we will, reminding us that they will do for

us what they are fitted to do only as we assume active responsibility for the use we make of them.

Authority then is fitted to serve us in the following ways. It can tell us what our predecessors have *thought* about God and so can help us to understand better what it is that we are to test for ourselves. It can remind us of what other men have *felt* about God and so furnish us with the motive for seeking the same kind of experience for ourselves.

CHAPTER IV

THE WAY OF INTUITION: OR MEETING GOD FACE TO FACE

1. The Element of Immediacy in Religious Experience.

   The Contribution of Intuition to Certainty—How the Intuitions of Religion Differ from Those of Common Life—What Intuition Contributes to Our Knowledge of God.

2. The Mystic's Attempt to Isolate God Through Abstraction from the World.

   What Is Meant by Mysticism—Positive and Negative Mysticism—Examples of Negative Mysticism—Its Limitations.

3. How Worship Helps Us to Recognize God's Presence in All Life.

   Baron von Hügel's Estimate of the Strength and Weakness of Classical Mysticism—The Mystical Element in Science and in Art—The Mystical Element in Ethics—The Function of the Classic as the Trysting Place of the Intuitions.

The second of the four ways of reaching certainty is through intuition, by which we mean those sudden insights, coming to us from time to time, which assure us that we are in immediate contact with some reality, inherently worthy. It is in response to such insights that all the great loyalties are born, whether their object be a person or a cause. The intuitions of religion differ from the intuitions of common life, not in their nature as a psychological process but in their object, which is God.

So fundamental is the part played by this aspect of our experience that many religious people have attempted to isolate it from the rest of life and to make it the sole ground for faith in God. We call those who practise this process of abstraction mystics. Some mystics have carried the process so far as to remove God from all contact not only with the world of sense perception but with that of thought as well. They base their assurance of his reality on an ineffable experience incapable of further definition. Others discover God's presence in specific objects in nature and in man which suggest qualities in deity which when once recognized they are afterwards able to discover in the world as a whole. We call such significant objects sacraments and their function is to serve as a meeting place for the intuitions.

1. THE ELEMENT OF IMMEDIACY IN RELIGIOUS EXPERIENCE

The Contribution of Intuition to Certainty

In the first chapter of the Fourth Gospel there is a passage[1] which tells how Jesus won one of his first disciples. It was through the contagion of personal contact. Nathaniel had heard his brother Philip telling of a new teacher whom he had met and who, he believed, might prove to be Israel's promised Messiah. But Nathaniel was not convinced. It was only when he met Jesus for himself and heard him speak words which struck home to his own conscience with irresistible conviction that he, too, became convinced of Jesus' divine mission and authority.

This is the way conviction always comes to us in the things that matter most. There is something mysterious about the experience we call faith, something creative and inexplicable that carries its own conviction with it. It comes to different people in different ways—sometimes in the most simple and natural way in the world, as when Jesus met Peter and John by the lake shore and called them to become fishers of men,[2] and, again, in some arresting crisis like the vision that came to Saul on the Damascus road and turned the persecutor into an apostle.[3] But however it comes, it carries with it always the

[1] John 1:43-51.   [2] Mark 1:16,17.   [3] Acts 9:1-9.

119

note of finality. If there has been doubt, there is now conviction; if there has been indecision, there is now certainty.

When I say that there is something mysterious about faith, I do not mean that there is anything magical about it. Faith is not a sixth sense by which we apprehend realities for which we have no other evidence. It is a capacity which we possess as human beings of appreciating the true significance of the realities with which we are in contact at all times. It is not a substitute for our other methods of knowledge. Rather is it our way of unifying what these other methods bring us piecemeal. Without faith, no one of the great convictions that make life worth living would be possible. The universe would be an endless succession of individual happenings without inner coherence or meaning, and human life would be a series of sensations, impulses, and emotions never attaining the dignity of a unity worthy to be called personal. Through the intuitions that come to us in our best moments we perceive the harmony in individual things and appreciate their value and their meaning with an immediacy possible in no other way.

So far as certainty comes to us at all in our most intimate and personal relationships, it comes to us in this way. How do I know that my friend is to be trusted, or that the woman I love is worthy of my love? Not because any one has told me that it is so, still less because I have weighed the arguments on one side or the other and come to a reasoned conclusion. I trust my friend, I love my wife, because I can-

not help it. There is something in me which goes out
to what I find in them with an irresistible impulse. I
love, I trust, so far as I love and trust at all, through
an intuition of faith.

In the preface contributed by Mr. Balfour to the
life of Alfred Lyttelton[4] there is a passage which
illustrates this quality of immediacy in human
friendship:

"I will not attempt any analysis of the unique charm
which makes the life of Alfred Lyttelton irreplaceable.
Such an attempt would indeed be vain. We can neither separate the whole into its parts, nor recompose the parts into
the whole. There was that about him which made immediate and irresistible appeal to every man and woman whom
he met, and made that appeal to what was best in them. . . .
Gaiety of spirit, humorous perception, delight in all things
that were lovely and of good report, he possessed in unique
measure; and these qualities made him the most charming of
playfellows. But none who knew him well ever lost the consciousness that his joy in life, and all that life can give, was
more than mere gaiety of temper. It was, in truth, the fair
flower of a pure character drawing its beauty from profound spiritual roots."[5]

What is true of our relationships to other persons
is true of our attitude to all the higher values of life:
our love of our country, for example, or our response
to beauty, or our sense of allegiance to the indefinable
obligations that we group together under the name
of duty, or of honor. Why are we sure that it is right
for us to feel toward these "imponderables" as we do
feel? It is because we cannot help ourselves. There

[4] *Alfred Lyttelton, An Account of His Life,* by Edith Lyttelton
(London, 1923).
[5] Page 13.

is something in us that says: This that I see is admirable; this that I feel is honorable; this that draws me with an inner constraint has the right so to draw me and I do well to yield to it, cost what it may. In all that makes life most worth living the intuition of faith speaks the last word.

How the Intuitions of Religion Differ from Those of Common Life

The intuitions of religion differ from the intuitions of common life, not in their nature as a psychological process, but in their object, which is God. What religious faith sees is not an individual person, but the one who is the source and standard of all true personality; not a particular value, but the being who is the summation and realization of all the values. Face to face with the problem of problems, whence come those qualities in human beings which draw us to them, how explain those elements in experience that make life glorious in spite of all its shame and tragedy, faith answers that they come from God, who is himself the secret source of the feelings of reverence and adoration which stir within us and the object in which alone they find their complete satisfaction.

The form which the conviction may take may differ widely according to the particular point of contact. Certainty has come to some men through the church, as when Augustine met Ambrose, the great Bishop of Milan, and became conscious for the first time of the spiritual significance of a majestic institution. To others it has come through the Bible, as when Luther read in the letter to the Galatians Paul's word, "The just shall live by faith," and was certain that in the words God was speaking to him. To still others it has come in the solitude of their own spirits, as when Finney, brooding over his sins, saw Christ standing before him so distinctly that he believed him to be physically present in the room;[6] or when Bushnell, perplexed as to his duty and doubting even the most fundamental truths of Christianity, saw clearly that, whatever else he might doubt, this at least was certain, that it was always right to do right.[7]

But however the form of the experience differs in other respects, it has been alike in this, that it has been an experience of certainty. The conviction which authority alone had failed to give, intuition has supplied. The doubts which reasoning had been powerless to dispel have vanished at a single flash of insight.

It was experience such as this that the writer of the Fourth Gospel had in mind when he reports Jesus' words concerning the Comforter who would

[6] "As I went in and shut the door after me, it seemed as if I met the Lord Jesus Christ face to face. It did not occur to me then, nor did it for some time afterward, that it was wholly a mental state. On the contrary it seemed to me that I saw him as I would see any other man. . . . I have always regarded this as a most remarkable state of mind; for it seemed to me a reality, that he stood before me, and I fell down at his feet and poured out my soul to him."—Finney, Charles G., *Memoirs* (New York, 1876), pp. 19–20.

[7] Munger, T. T., *Horace Bushnell, Preacher and Theologian* (Boston, 1899), pp. 23-27, esp. p. 26.

lead the disciples into all truth.[8] It was the certainty which such experience brings that gave our Puritan fathers confidence when they spoke of the witness of the Spirit.[9]

What Intuition Contributes to Our Knowledge of God

Many different questions may arise as to the nature and origin of the experience of certainty. Some of them, as we have seen, are psychological and have to do with the conditions in ourselves or in our environment which make it possible. Others are logical and have to do with its trustworthiness when it is here. We are not concerned here primarily with questions of the first kind. They are a part of the wider question how all our conscious life takes place, and more particularly how far the deterministic assumptions of our modern scientific procedure are applicable in the sphere of the personal self-conscious life. We are interested in the more immediate and practical question how far our intuitions, however we explain their origin, may be trusted to give us knowledge of reality.

That depends in part upon our definition of reality. If we confine reality solely to the objects of sense perception, the immediate impressions that come to us from the universe, we shall of course answer the question in the negative. But if we recognize, as most philosophers recognize, and almost all normal people

[8] John 16: 12.
[9] Westminster Confession of Faith, chap. I, v.

when they are not trying to philosophize, that the world of values and of meanings is as real in its own way as the world of sense, we shall have no difficulty in believing that our intuitions, which are concerned with values and with meanings, have an indispensable contribution to make to our knowledge of the real world.[10]

Indeed so far is it from being true that those who have thought most deeply about the mystery of life regard the realm of values as less real than the world of sense that on the contrary there are philosophers who contend that, if by value we understand all those qualities in things and relations between them which transform our world from a collection of meaningless data into an intelligible universe, the world of value is the *only* real world. The idealists of all schools have inclined to this view. Professor Santayana has suggested a name for these objects of immediate certainty. He calls them essences.[11] Essences, as he defines them, are the inherent qualities and relations which give meaning to every possible world of experience, whether it is realized in fact or not.[12] As such they are the object of mathematics and of logic and of those more abstract aspects of philosophy which are concerned with necessary relationships. The contemplation of these ideal objects may call forth a very real satisfaction of an æsthetic kind.

[10] Professor Dewey himself thus defines the problem of philosophy in our modern empirical age: "What shall we do to make *objects having value* more secure in existence?" (italics mine). (*The Quest for Certainty*, p. 43.)

[11] *The Realm of Essence* (New York, 1927).

[12] Pages 18-25.

Even if they admit of no closer personal relationship they may be made the object of religious worship, as Mr. Bertrand Russell has shown in his essays, *A Free Man's Worship* and *The Study of Mathematics*.[13]

It is not of this highly abstract realm, however, that the plain man is thinking when he tells us of the insights which have come to him. He is not concerned with qualities which may possibly be realized in some as yet non-existent object but with the qualities he finds in living men or discovers in some historic cause. It was not for justice in the abstract that men fought in the great war but for justice as they conceived it to be embodied in the specific objects for which their countries were fighting. And it was this faith more than their guns and their munitions which, if we are to believe Marshal Foch, in the last analysis gave victory to the Allies. "Is it not curious," he asks, "to see moral force, idealism, all that is finest and greatest in man, animating peoples at war and leading them irresistibly to victory? What then makes this invincible force? At bottom, the absolute certainty that one defends a just and sacred cause; in the execution, the sustained energy of all, upheld by a common sentiment of justice and liberty."[14]

But there are victories of the spirit more significant than those won over armies and navies, the victories that men have won over cowardice and pride and greed. In a recent autobiography, one of the

[13] In *Philosophical Essays* (London, 1920), pp. 59-86.
[14] Foch, quoted by Recouly in New York *Times*, May 26, 1929.

participants in the great war has described such a
victory:

"It was during my first night in France on my way to
Vimy Ridge in April 1917 that [Jesus] vindicated for me
my hope that when everything else failed He would stand
sure. I am perhaps physically and certainly morally a cow-
ard; . . . and when death looked me in the face, my man-
hood withered and collapsed. For what seemed hours I was
in an agony of fear. Men talked of honor and a flag—I
would have forsworn any earthly loyalty for the bare gift
of life; or of immortality when one yearns for the dear
small familiar things of earth, and the clutch of a baby's
fingers on one's hand, and the smile in a woman's eyes; or
of sacrifice and heroism, fine themes for talk, but poor con-
solation if all one's dreams are to end in a shattered pulp
of blood and brain; or of God—and suddenly as if spoken
in the very room His words, 'For their sakes I consecrate
myself,' and the fragrant splendor of His presence.
"I was overwrought, no doubt. The day had been too
great a strain. . . . Maybe the visualizing of the Lord was
due to my mental state; maybe the words were my own
rendering of His impact; but for the next nine months He
was never absent, and I never alone, and never save for an
instant or two broken by fear. If He who was with me when
I was blown up by a shell, and gassed, and sniped at, with
me in hours of bombardment and the daily walk of death,
was an illusion, then all that makes life worth living for me
is illusion too; and I can only thank God that in this mock-
ery of existence there has been a dream so beautiful, so
realistic, so potent in its effects."[15]

It was not only among the Allies that such victories were won. Many a young German, responding
loyally to his country's call, and confident that her
cause was just, faced the same inner conflict and was

[15] Raven, Charles E., *A Wanderer's Way* (New York, 1929),
pp. 202-204.

sustained by a like faith—faith in one who speaks through the call of duty and who gives strength to meet the call when it comes.

It is such faith as this with which the intuitions of religion are concerned; not faith in God in the abstract, but faith in a God immediately known in personal experience as disclosing his will to individuals and to groups in ways that admit of recognition. This is what immanence means when translated from the language of philosophy into that of religion. Not that God is present everywhere in the universe, true though that be, but that God is so present in his world that we can recognize his presence at specific times and in definite places, and the avenue through which that recognition comes is intuition.[16]

2. The Mystic's Attempt to Isolate God through Abstraction from the World

What Is Meant by Mysticism

Intuition, then, is the name we give to those recurrent insights which assure us of the reality of God. So fundamental is this service of our intuitions that,

[16] Calvin is not a theologian of whom we think as over-emphasizing the pragmatic aspect of religion. Yet in his *Institutes* he expressed his view of the function of theology in these words:
"Those . . . who . . . propose to inquire what the essence of God is only delude us with frigid speculations—it being much more our interest to know what kind of being God is, and what things are agreeable to his nature. For of what use is it to join Epicurus in acknowledging some God who has cast off the care of the world, and only delights himself in ease? What avails it, in short, to know a God with whom we have nothing to do?"—(Eng. tr. by Beveridge (Edinburgh, 1845), vol. I, p. 52.)

as we have seen, men have been tempted to isolate the intuitive element in experience from its setting and to treat it as an independent source of knowledge. It is not only the philosophers who have made this attempt. Religious men also have made it, and they have made it in the name of religion.

The name which is generally given to this attempt is mysticism. In mystical religion God is completely separated from the world of form and color, of motion and change, of number and relation, sometimes even of right and wrong, from which alone we gain the symbols by which we fill up our idea of God with content. God becomes a nameless presence, too august to be defined, even to be described, only to be realized in the incommunicable thrill that comes to the worshipper who surrenders himself completely to his spell in the silence of the Spirit.

So important is the rôle which mysticism has played in the history of religion that it is desirable to consider it in some detail. This is the easier because in recent years a number of studies have been made of the mystical experience, not only by those who are attracted to it for religious reasons but by psychologists and philosophers, whose interest is primarily scientific. The best known example is Professor William James' well-known Gifford Lectures on *The Varieties of Religious Experience*. But he is only one of many who could be named.[17]

---

[17] *E. g.*, Leuba, James H., *The Psychology of Religious Mysticism* (New York, 1925); Bennett, Charles A., *A Philosophical Study of Mysticism* (New Haven, 1923); Royce, Josiah, *The World and the Individual* (New York, 1901).

One reason for this new interest in mysticism on the part of those who have had little sympathy with the non-rational type of religion is the discovery of the large part which is played in our life by our emotions. So much is this the case that, as we have seen, there is a tendency among psychologists to regard many of our most cherished convictions as rationalizations, that is, reasons invented after the fact, to justify decisions reached on other grounds. To those who take this view of the nature of our conscious life, the experience of the mystics, with their vivid sense of a certainty for which no completely rational grounds can be given, brings interesting material for investigation.

The recent increase of interest in mystical religion has also a more practical ground. The growing complexity of life with its demand upon people for sudden decisions, the breakdown of authority in its older and more conventional forms, with its inevitable consequences in uncertainty and doubt, have led many to turn their thoughts within in quest of the assurance they need. To all who are seeking a refuge from the strain of life, the mystic way promises a means of escape. These seekers lend a ready ear when their predecessors in the quest tell them of a peace possible here and now for those who turn away from the seen world and seek the light which is within.

This concentration upon God as the supreme fact, as distinct from all the special facts which suggest his presence, is known as worship. In worship we turn aside a moment from the finite world in which

most of our life is lived and fix our attention upon
the abiding realities which outlast all change of time
or outward circumstance. The exaltation of spirit
which comes through such withdrawal is the worshipper's assurance that it is God with whom he has to do.
For the devotees of the mystical life, worship is the
dominant interest.

Positive and Negative Mysticism

In the broadest sense mysticism is used to designate
the element of immediacy in man's consciousness of
God, however that consciousness may be mediated in
detail. Thus Wordsworth is called a nature-mystic
because of his vivid sense of the immanence of God in
nature, and Hegel's attempt to see in all history the
outworking of one unfolding divine plan has been regarded as evidence of a mystical strain in his philosophy. Most frequently, however, the term mysticism is restricted to the experience of those who rely
for their certainty wholly on an inner non-rational
revelation.

An example of this attempt to contrast God's presence with every concrete fact which evidences it is the
familiar passage in the Westminster Confession of
Faith in which its authors state the reason for their
certainty that the Bible is indeed the word of God:

"Although we may be moved and induced by the testimony of the Church to an high and reverent esteem of the
Holy Scripture, and the heavenliness of the matter, the
efficacy of the doctrine, the majesty of the style, the consent
of all the parts, the scope of the whole (which is to give
all glory to God) the full discovery it makes of the only

way of man's salvation, the many other incomparable excellencies, and the entire perfection thereof, are arguments whereby it doth abundantly evidence itself to be the Word of God. Yet notwithstanding our full persuasion and assurance of the infallible truth and divine authority thereof, is from the inward work of the Holy Spirit, bearing witness by and with the Word in our hearts."[18]

A parallel to the Westminster doctrine of the witness of the Spirit is found in the dogmatic decrees of the Vatican Council. After speaking of the function of reason in religion, the Fathers go on to declare that faith is superior to reason even in the sphere where reason operates. This faith, "which is the beginning of man's salvation," is "a supernatural virtue, whereby, inspired and assisted by the grace of God, we believe that the things which he has revealed are true; not because of the intrinsic truth of the things, viewed by the natural light of reason, but because of the authority of God himself, who reveals them, and who can neither be deceived nor deceive."[19]

There are analogies in common life which in a measure explain, even if they do not wholly justify, this contrast. We all know what it means to hear a familiar passage read until we know it by heart, without its ever awakening any inner response within us, and then suddenly—we know not how or why—on the next repetition some responsive note is struck, some inner contact is made, and we say, "Yes, I see. Now I understand." This difference between sight and insight, the hearing of the ear and the understanding

[18] Westminster Confession of Faith, I:v.
[19] *Creeds of Christendom,* Schaff, Philip, vol. II, chap. III, p. 243.

of the mind, is the fact of experience which gives us our clue to the understanding of what the mystics tell us.

But when we go further and try to separate the two aspects of our experience completely we become involved in difficulties. What intuition does, as we have seen,[1] is not to give us knowledge otherwise wholly unattainable; rather to interpret to us the meaning of the knowledge already open to us. Neither in the case of Bible or of church is it possible to carry out in fact the complete separation which the theory assumes. It is the Spirit which bears witness, to be sure, but that to which it witnesses is the Bible, or, to be more exact, the truth which the Bible contains; this particular concrete book, with the qualities the critics describe, the antecedents the historians record, and the teaching the theologians expound. It is because it contains such elements and no other that it produces the effect that it does and wins the assent it calls forth. And this is true in greater or less degree of all the other objects to which faith responds. It is true of the church. It is true of Jesus Christ. It is true supremely of God, who reveals himself in and through all three.

Examples of Negative Mysticism

The great mystics, to be sure, have not been satisfied with this account of their experience. They tell us of an immediacy even more immediate, a certainty still more certain; and this they find in an ineffable

[1] *Cf.* p. 20.

experience, incapable of further description, only to be known by him to whom it comes. To win this certainty they have often subjected themselves to the most rigorous discipline, denied themselves enjoyments lawful to ordinary men, spent long nights in vigil and long days in prayer; and they tell us that from time to time their efforts have been rewarded and that they have had the ineffable joy of meeting God face to face.

But they cannot describe to others that which they have seen and felt in these ecstatic moments. "This is the peculiarity of the divine language," writes Saint John of the Cross, one of the ablest of all the mystical writers:

"The more infused, intimate, spiritual, and supersensible it is, the more does it exceed the senses, both inner and outer, and impose silence upon them. . . . The soul then feels as if placed in a vast and profound solitude, to which no created thing has access, in an immense and boundless desert, desert the more delicious the more solitary it is. There, in this abyss of wisdom, the soul grows by what it drinks in from the well-springs of the comprehension of love. . . . and recognizes, however sublime and learned may be the terms we employ, how utterly vile, insignificant, and improper they are, when we seek to discourse of divine things by their means."[20]

Sometimes the separation between God and the world is carried to almost unbelievable lengths, as in this passage from an ancient apologist:

"If you do not refuse to hear what we think, we are so far from attributing to God bodily lineaments that we fear

[20] Quoted in James, *The Varieties of Religious Experience* (New York, 1902), pp. 407, 408.

to ascribe to so great an object even the graces of the mind, and the very virtues in which to excel is hardly granted to a few. For who can speak of God as brave, as constant, as moderate, as wise. Nay, who can say that He knows anything, that He understands, that He acts with foresight, that He directs the determination of His actions towards definite ends of duty. These are human goods, and as opposed to vices deserve a laudable reputation. But who is there so dull of heart and stupid as to call God great in human goods, or to speak of the surpassing excellence of His name as if it consisted in a freedom from the stain of vices. Whatever you can say of God, whatever you can conceive in silent thought, passes into a human sense, and is corrupted thereby. Nothing can properly signify and denote Him which is expressed in terms of human speech for human uses. There is but one way in which man can understand with certainty concerning the nature of God, and that is to know and feel that nothing can be expressed concerning Him in mortal speech."[21]

Its Limitations

What shall we say of such a religious experience? This first, that, to him who has it, it does indeed bring the assurance and comfort that he needs. Certainty has come to many a troubled spirit in this way.

[21]Arnobius, *adv. Gentes,* iii, 19, quoted in Mansel, *Limits of Religious Thought,* 5th ed., 1867, p. 22.

An interesting modern parallel to this conception of God, as a being only to be described by his contrast to man, is found in the theology of Karl Barth and his disciples. These theologians of Crisis, as they are called, criticize the mystical approach to God as "bringing him too close to [man] to be really [his] Lord." But when they in their turn attempt to define God they have recourse to the same negative terminology which is the stock in trade of the mystic. God "is the other one, the mysterious and unknowable One, who has his own proper name, and whom we do not know, because he is person. He reveals himself as the unheard-of, unrecognized mysterious person who cannot be discovered anywhere in the world." *Cf.* Brunner, H. Emil, *The Theology of Crisis* (New York, 1929), pp. 30, 31.

But such certainty has two drawbacks. The experience from which it is derived does not last and the knowledge that it brings cannot be shared.

The experience does not last. All students of mysticism agree with William James that one of the characteristics of the mystical state is its transiency.[22] It comes and goes, and one can never be sure when it will return. If what it brought could be shared this transiency would be no great drawback. But where the knowledge imparted is ineffable, the situation is altered. How can one tell whether what was learned is to be trusted unless it can be put in such form as to admit of some continuing social test?

This brings us to the second difficulty with the mystic's way of knowing. It is not only that the experience from which he derives his knowledge cannot be repeated at will. The knowledge it brings cannot be shared. And so the farther he goes in the knowledge of God, the farther he is separated from his fellowmen.

There is a passage in Baron von Hügel's life of St. Catherine of Genoa, which I have elsewhere quoted,[23] which admirably illustrates the elusive character of the mystic's experience. Speaking of the saint's experience of ecstasy, the Baron tells us that under the stress of her emotion she would cry: "Oh, would I could tell what my heart feels!" And her children would say: "Oh, mother, tell us something of it."

[22] *The Varieties of Religious Experience*, p. 381.
[23] *The Life of Prayer in a World of Science* (New York, 1927), p. 119.

And she would answer: "I cannot find words appropriate to so great a love. But this I can say with truth, that if of what my heart feels one drop were to fall into hell, hell itself would altogether turn into Eternal Life."[24]

Even for this most sublimated form of the mystical experience there is something to be said. If while it lasts it does not give us definite knowledge, it may help us to reach the place where definite knowledge is to be had. Professor Wieman has recently emphasized this service of the mystical experience in a suggestive essay, which has had the approval of no less an authority than Professor Dewey. One of our greatest difficulties, Professor Wieman points out, is that we become the slave of our habits. We do over again from day to day the things that we have done before. Our thoughts, like horses in a treadmill, keep tramping up and down in the same narrow enclosure without bringing us a step farther forward. What are we to do in a situation like this? We must interrupt the course of thought altogether. We must break with the habits we have formed at any cost; and this complete interruption, this radical break, the mystical experience makes possible. When it is over we come back to the familiar world of every day with rested mind and fresh courage and see things that we have never seen before.[25]

---

[24] *The Mystical Element of Religion as Studied in St. Catherine of Genoa and Her Friends* (London, 1908), vol. I, p. 159.

[25] "Religion in Dewey's Experience and Nature," *The Journal of Religion*, vol. X, 1925, pp. 519–541. *Cf.* esp. pp. 553 f. "One of the great values of mysticism . . . is that it enables us to escape

But the great mystics have claimed more than this for their experience. They tell us of moments when they have received definite revelations concerning God, and salvation, and duty. Saint Theresa tells us that she learned to understand the Trinity![26] Others have told of their experience of the risen Christ. To still others divine messages have come telling them to do this or that, and, in not a few cases, important consequences have followed from their obedience to the divine command. One thinks of the Apostle Paul's experience on the Damascus road, and it can be paralleled by many another. Yet when we inquire as to the exact nature of the communication which has been vouchsafed, in order to discover how far it deals with matters wholly novel and unfamiliar, we find that in almost every case we can discover some contact with the subject's earlier experience that supplies the material to which the new insight lends fresh meaning. If Saint Theresa had not known something about the Trinity before she entered upon her quest

from such a hard outer shell of meaning. The mystic experience is a meaningless conscious event. In mysticism we discard all our old meanings, and consciously submerge ourselves in the total event of experience. Out of such an experience we may emerge in a mental state which develops new meanings or modifies and reinterprets the old meanings and readapts them to the events of space-time."

[26] " 'How this vision comes to pass,' she says, 'I know not; but it does come to pas, and the three Persons of the Holy Trinity then show themselves to the soul with a radiance as of fire, which, like a shining cloud, first invades the mind and admirably illuminates it. Then she sees those three distinct Persons, and she knows with a sovereign truth that these three are One in substance, One in Power, One in wisdom, One God: so that those things which we know in this world by faith, the soul, in this light, understands by a sort of vision which is neither the vision of the body nor that of the soul; for it is not a sensible vision."—(Quoted in Underhill, Evelyn, *Mysticism*, 5th ed. (London, 1914), p. 132.)

of sainthood she would not have recognized the revelation that came to her in the mystic state as a revelation of the Trinity. So unless Saul during his life as a persecutor had learned something about Jesus he would never have known whose voice it was that came to him on the Damascus road.

We are confirmed, therefore, in the conviction with which we started, that intuition fulfils its true function when it is regarded not as a substitute for other knowledge but as its confirmation and interpretation. Far from its being true that mystical experience accentuates the distance between God and his world, it actually brings them nearer. Now, after it has come, we are able to see him where we could not have seen him before.

3. How Worship Helps Us to Recognize God's Presence in All Life

Baron von Hügel's Estimate of the Strength and Weakness of Classical Mysticism

Thus it would appear that our intuitions, whether we think of them in the more familiar forms in which they make part of the experience of every day or in those rarer and more exceptional forms in which they have been granted to the great religious spirits of our race, do most for us when we think of them not as standing alone but as an indispensable help in the use of the other pathways to certainty that we have still to study. This is the conclusion reached by Baron von Hügel, himself one of the wisest of recent stu-

dents of mysticism. In a letter written to Father
Tyrrell, under date of September 26, 1898, he sums
up his conclusion on this much-debated subject as
follows: In four points he finds the mystics certainly in the right; but in a fifth, the negative world-re-
nouncing attitude we have been studying, he feels
constrained to part company with them.

They are right, he tells us, "perfectly right," when
they tell us that:

"God, our own souls, all the supreme realities and truths
. . . are both *incomprehensible* and *indefinitely apprehen-
sible,* and the constant vivid realization of these two qualities . . . inherent to all our knowledge and practice of
them, is of primary and equal importance for us."

(2) They are right, further, when they remind
us that our apprehension of the divine is morally conditioned:

"This indefinite apprehensibleness becomes an actual
ever-increasing apprehension, more through the purification
of the heart than through the exercise of the reason, and
without some [such] experience . . . the reason has no
adequate material for effective conclusions."

(3) Still again, they are right in insisting that:

"The primary function of religion is not the consoling of
the natural man as it finds him, but the purification of this
man, by effecting an ever-growing cleavage and contrast
between his bad false self . . . and his true good self . . .;
and the deepest . . . aspirations of every human heart,"
confused and dumb though they be, "correspond exactly to,
and come from precisely the same source, as the external
helps and examples of miracle, Church or Saint. The true
exceptional is thus never the queer, but the supremely nor-

mal, and but embodies, in an exceptional degree, the deepest, and hence exceptional longings of us all."

(4) Finally, they are right in recognizing that this purification of the lower self:

"must take place by man voluntarily plunging into some purifying bath or medium of a kind necessarily painful to the false, surface, immediate, animal man, and necessarily purifying where willed and accepted by the true, inner, remoter, spiritual self."[27]

Such a purifying bath the mystics find in the process of abstraction through which they withdraw their attention from all that is concrete and particular in their experience. But when they go further and make abstraction the sole method of approach to God they go astray. To teach, as many of the great mystics do, that we come to know God truly only as we turn aside from the concrete, familiar world of every day and become more and more absorbed in the general is not only to leave no place for "experimental, observing science" but to weaken, if not altogether to destroy, the motive for reform in the actual world.

Both activities, the world-denying and the world-affirming, the Baron therefore concludes, should be united in every normal human experience. They will be combined in different degrees in different people and at different times in the life of the same person, but neither should exclude the other. On the contrary, they should be combined both in theory and in

[27] *Selected Letters*, von Hügel, Baron F., pp. 71, 22 (London, Toronto, and New York, 1927).

practice in indissoluble unity. For in the study of
the concrete world of fact, as science understands it,

"God . . . has given us . . . a purifying medium, which
as many will and ought to use as have, in the past, striven
to use the medium of abstraction alone." . . . [It follows
that] every man should "be taught in Retreats that he must
study or work at something definite and concrete, not simply to escape the dangers of idleness or to take off the strain
of direct spirituality, but because, without them, he will, as
we now know and see things, avoid one of the two twin
means of growing lowly and pure, and of removing himself
from the centre of his (otherwise little) world."[28]

The Mystical Element in Science and in Art

No one who has observed the life of the great scientists can question the truth of Baron von Hügel's
judgment. There is about them a simplicity and sin-
gleness of mind, a subordination of all that is personal and selfish to the supreme end in view, that reminds us of the lives of the great saints. To them, too,
intuitions come of truth and of beauty that lift them
up above all that is transient and fleeting into the
realm of the eternal. But the God they there see is
not a distant God but the same mysterious presence
whose footsteps in star-dust and light rays they have
been retracing through the laborious process of experiment and calculation that have gone into the
making of the physics and the astronomy of to-day.

In a remarkable autobiographical passage in which
he describes an experience of his own, in which a complicated mathematical law was instantly revealed to

[28] *Op. cit.*, p. 73.

him, M. Henri Poincaré, the distinguished French mathematician, calls attention to the æsthetic quality in mathematical intuitions:

"It may appear surprising that sensibility should be introduced in connection with mathematical demonstrations, which, it would seem, can only interest the intellect. But not if we bear in mind the feeling of mathematical beauty, of the harmony of numbers and forms and of geometric elegance. It is a real æsthetic feeling that all true mathematicians recognize, and this is truly sensibility.

"Now, what are the mathematical entities to which we attribute this character of beauty and elegance, which are capable of developing in us a kind of æsthetic emotion? Those whose elements are harmoniously arranged so that the mind can, without effort, take in the whole without neglecting the details. This harmony is at once a satisfaction to our æsthetic requirements, and an assistance to the mind which it supports and guides. At the same time, by setting before our eyes a well-ordered whole, it gives us a presentiment of a mathematical law."[29]

What the scientists discover of God in the pursuit of truth is revealed to the artists and poets in their quest of beauty. They, too, use common tools to reveal to us uncommon things, and the medium in which they work is the medium in which all our life is lived, —that oldest and most constant of our companions which even the most materialistic of our contemporaries in moments when they are off their guard cannot help personifying as Mother Nature. They too look past the things the physical eye sees to the things that eye hath not seen nor ear heard, even the things that God hath prepared for those that love him; and

[29] *Science and Method,* Eng. tr. (New York), p. 59.

they bring us news of what they have discovered in words that wake an answering echo in our hearts. Wordsworth tells us how in the presence of some familiar scene:

> "the soul
> Put off her veil, and self-transmuted, stood,
> Naked, as in the presence of her God."

He recalls hours when

> "The sea lay laughing at a distance; near
> The solid mountains shone, bright as the clouds,
> Grain-tinctured, drenched in empyrean light,
> And on the meadows and the lower ground,
> Was all the sweetness of a common dawn—
> Dews, vapors, and the melody of birds,
> And laborers going forth to till the fields.
>
> .   .   .   .
>
> My heart was full. I made no vows; but vows
> Were then made for me; bond unknown to me
> Was given, that I should be, else sinning greatly,
> A dedicated spirit. On I walked
> In thankful blessedness, which yet survives."[30]

"Which yet survives." It is the last sentence which is significant. These intuitions of the poets claim our serious attention just because they are not merely transient. Their effects last on in those to whom they have happened and in us to whom the story is told.

It is not only nature mystics like Wordsworth who recognize a persistent quality in the true mystical revelation which outlasts the transiency of the mystical state. This continuing element is emphasized in an illuminating passage from Saint Theresa which

[30] *Prelude,* pp. 259-261, Morley's edition (New York, 1889).

William James quotes in his *Varieties of Religious Experience*. "If you ask," the Saint writes, "how it is possible that the soul can see and understand that she has been in God, since during the union she has neither sight nor understanding, I reply that she does not see it then, but that she sees it clearly later, after she has returned to herself, not by any vision, but by a certitude which abides with her and which God alone can give her."

"But how, you will repeat, *can* one have such certainty in respect to what one does not see? This question, I am powerless to answer. These are secrets of God's omnipotence which it does not appertain to me to penetrate. All that I know is that I tell the truth; and I shall never believe that any soul who does not possess this certainty has ever been really united to God."[31]

Thus even the technical mystics who are continually emphasizing the transiency of the mystical state fall back at last upon one at least of the tests on which the plain man must rely for his assurance—the lasting quality of the insight which it brings.

The Mystical Element in Ethics

One more point of contact Baron von Hügel makes which has played a great rôle in the history of religion and which in Christianity has come to occupy the central place—the fact of human need, which has been the challenge of religion in all ages and which sets the disciple his task of reform, first of himself, then of others. God is present in nature, but he is

[31] Pp. 409, 410.

present even more characteristically in man, and it is from the latter revelation alone that the true secret of his nature is to be learned. With our intuitions of truth and of beauty there come also intuitions of goodness and of duty. In a world without men and women the lesson of God's love would hardly have been learned.

We are not dealing here with theoretical considerations; we are simply recounting facts. Wordsworth could see God in impersonal things like mountains and lakes, but he hailed duty as a "stern daughter of the voice of God." Jesus drew lessons from God's care for flowers and birds, but he reminded his disciples that they were of more value than many sparrows. If we ask when men have been most vividly conscious of God, the answer must be that it is when they have come into contact with men and women who have done justice and loved mercy and walked humbly with their God. It is through Jesus and the great characters whose spirits have been formed by him that we are able most clearly to discover God's presence in his world and to anticipate the time when all humanity shall be completely the organ of his Spirit as exceptional individuals are to-day.

Indeed it is only when we touch this ethical element that we reach that which is central in the Christian conception of God. Jesus worshipped the Creator of the universe, who is known to us through our intuitions of beauty and of wonder. But Jesus revealed God to us more intimately as the Father of our Spirits, who cares for each one of us, even when we go astray, and who seeks through his participation in our human experiences to win us to his ideal of love.

Not the least of our debts to humanism is its re-emphasis upon the ethical element in human life. Beauty has its revelation to the sensitive spirit, but the love which unites man with his fellows brings us still closer to the heart of things.

The Function of the Classic as the Trysting Place of the Intuitions

Our intuitions then are responses to a real world of things and of persons. Yet we must face this singular fact, that while all nature is vocal with God and though all history evidences his presence, not all parts of nature speak to us with equal distinctness nor is his presence equally manifest at all times in history. There are some objects which have a revealing quality which is not present in others. They not only appeal to more persons but they maintain their influence over longer periods of time. Such an object is Jesus. Such an object is the Bible, which speaks of Jesus. Such an object is the church, through which the mission of Jesus is continued. These are symbols which witness to us of realities which are unseen.

And not to us only but to others also. They remind us of what others before us have seen and heard of God. For there is this significant thing about our intuitions, that while of all our experiences they are the most private and personal they are not on that account exclusively our own. On the contrary, they point us to realities which are apprehended by others than ourselves, and so make possible a fellowship which of all fellowships is the most intimate and sacred.

At this point the two paths which we have thus far been following separately meet on a common high road. As authority led us on to intuition, so intuition points us back to authority. Neither is complete without the other. In the union of the two we find the most direct and reliable of the ways of approach to God.

Authority adds to the witness of intuition two elements of great importance—universality and permanence. We trust our own judgments concerning truth or beauty in part because they are shared by other persons. We trust them still more because they last. What we call a classic in literature or in art is an object which has called forth response from multitudes of people and has continued to call it forth through the changes in the years. It is the trysting place of the intuitions, a place where spirit meets spirit in the thrill of a great affection or of a compelling loyalty.

The objects which call forth such response, as we have seen, are of many different kinds. Some men find the supreme object of their loyalty in a person, others in a book, still others in an institution which comes to them as the custodian of an ancient tradition and in ritual acts which speak to the emotions and dramatize the truths to which they witness. But whether the response be to a person, or to a book, or to an institution, the effect is the same,—a clear-cut conviction as to duty or destiny, to which faith responds with complete confidence as guaranteeing the certainty we need.

It is in intuition then—the immediate insight that comes to us from time to time—that for the first time we find the assurance we need. If only we could see as clearly all the time as we do in our best moments; if only what we see others could see also, we should need no further evidence and our quest for certainty would be at an end.

But, alas, we do not. Insight comes and goes. Vision fades. What seemed crystal clear yesterday has become obscure to-day. And when the next flash comes what we then see may not agree with what we saw before. Even in ourselves intuitions differ.

And if in ourselves, how much more in others. The perplexing fact is not simply that we ourselves are not always sure but that different people are so often equally sure about different things.

What shall we do when our insights fail us or when they conflict with the insight of others whom we recognize as better and wiser than ourselves? From the difficulty of differing authorities we may turn to intuition for deliverance. But where shall we find the test by which to judge between differing intuitions?

There are two possible tests which we may use. One is the test of consistency, the other that of adaptability. We may ask which of the competing beliefs best explains the other known facts of our world, or we may ask which will prove best able to adjust itself to the changes which the future has in store. The first of these tests we may call the method of reasoning, the second the method of experiment. They are the third and the fourth of our pathways to certainty.

CHAPTER V

THE WAY OF REASONING: OR THE TEST OF CONSISTENCY

1. The Approach Through Reasoning.

What Is Meant by Reasoning—The Arguments for the Being of God—The Permanent Significance of the Arguments—Why Many No Longer Find the Arguments Convincing.

2. Difficulties Raised by Physical Science.

Contrast Between the Old World and the New—Danger of Exaggerating the Contrast—The Symbolic Character of Language—The Difficulty of Magnitude—The Difficulty of Determinism.

3. How Science Helps Us to Meet the Difficulties It Raises.

The Growing Recognition of Unity—The Growing Appreciation of Value—The New Admission of Mobility—What Reasoning Can Do for Us and What It Cannot Do.

4. The Difficulty Presented by the Fact of Evil.

The Difficulty Stated—How the Philosophers Have Dealt with the Problem of Evil—Where the Solution of Philosophy Is Inadequate.

In the broadest sense reasoning is the name which we give to any process by which we validate conviction. In the narrower sense it is the process through which from data immediately given we make inferences as to the nature of some object of which we have no direct knowledge. The most familiar examples of the use of this method in religion are the well-known arguments for the being of God. These arguments reason from the contingency of the universe and from its adaptation to human need to the existence of a wise and beneficent creator. In our own day their validity has been challenged, partly on the ground that they cannot demonstrate the kind of God that religion postulates, partly on the ground that they ignore evidence equally accessible which is inconsistent with the existence of such a God.

So far as the first contention is concerned, it is to be said that while the arguments cannot give us a demonstration of the existence of God, they call attention to qualities in the universe which have made it seem reasonable to religious people to believe in the existence of a good God. So far as the second objection is concerned it is further to be said that while there is much in our present world that seems inconsistent with the existence of such a God, religious faith explains the presence of these disturbing factors as a necessary element in a process of discipline which is not yet complete.

1. The Approach Through Reasoning

What Is Meant by Reasoning

The third of the possible pathways to certainty is reasoning. The word may be used in a broader and in a narrower sense. In the broadest sense it is the name we give to any process by which we validate conviction. So defined it includes all four of the methods we have been studying so far as they admit of any other test than the immediate satisfaction they give. In the narrower sense it is the process by which we infer from data which are immediately given, either by sense perception or intuition, conclusions as to the nature of some object of which we have no direct knowledge.[1]

In this chapter we shall be primarily concerned with reasoning in the narrower sense, although it will not be possible wholly to ignore its broader uses.

When a man makes statements about something of which I have no first-hand knowledge, the most direct

---

[1] In his suggestive book, *The Function of Reason* (Princeton, 1929), Professor Alfred Whitehead distinguishes two functions of reason, one speculative, the other practical. "The speculative reason is in its essence untrammeled by method. Its function is to pierce into the general reasons beyond limited reasons, to understand all methods as co-ordinated in a nature of things only to be grasped by transcending all method" (p. 51). The practical reason on the other hand is "reason criticizing and emphasizing the subordinate purposes in nature which are the agents of final causation" (p. 23).

What Professor Whitehead here calls the speculative reason is substantially what we have elsewhere described as intuition, whereas reasoning in the narrow sense in which we shall use the word in this chapter is the tool which the practical reason uses in the accomplishment of its utilitarian task.

and convincing way to assure myself that he has spoken the truth is to go to the source from which he derived his information that I may test it for myself. With many objects in the external world this is a comparatively simple matter—at least in principle. If I am told that a certain trunk weighs one hundred and twenty pounds, I put it on the scales and read the indicator. If I am told that a bill I hold in my hand is worth ten silver dollars, I take it to the bank and receive ten dollars in exchange. But with many matters with which we are concerned such a direct and easy way is not possible. We have no scales at hand that are big enough to hold the weight we wish to test and the bank is too far away for us to go in person to cash our check. Here we have to resort to indirect methods. We reason from the effects that we see to the cause which is likely to have produced them. And from the comparison of many different elements, each in itself insufficient to carry conviction, we win certainty.

Much of our knowledge of the physical universe is gained in this way. This is the way in which we learn of the speed of light or of the size of the sun. The more startling results reached in recent physics, with their revolutionary transformation of our conception of the constitution of the atom or of the variation in the length of objects caused by changes in their rate of motion, have been obtained in this way. From data that lie within the range of our observation and measurement we draw conclusions as to the nature of objects to which we have no direct access.

If it is necessary to use the method of inference in dealing with objects that are known to us through sense perception, how much more necessary must it be for us to make use of inference when we are dealing with such a belief as the existence of God? God is not a material fact that can be touched or seen or handled. We cannot put him on the scales to be weighed, or take him to the bank to be cashed. He is himself the scale by which we weigh, the bank at which we cash. If we believe in him it must be because we have found evidence of his existence in the effects which he has produced and is producing in the world about us and in our own lives. And such effects, as a matter of fact, religious men have believed themselves to find in the beauty with which the world is clothed, the meaning it reveals, and the way in which it lends itself to the realization of our purposes. The description of these effects and the conclusions which it is reasonable to draw from them make up what are known in theology as the arguments for the being of God.

The Arguments for the Being of God

It is not necessary here to restate these arguments in detail. Suffice it to say that they take their departure from observed phenomena in the universe and in man, and reason from them to a cause which is adequate to produce them. From the fact that we are living in a changing world it is argued that there must be some cause adequate to produce the change. From the fact that the world lends itself to the realization of our purposes it is inferred that there must be a purposing mind to account for the adaptation. From the presence of spiritual ideals and values the conclusion is drawn that the cause which has produced them must itself have the qualities of meaning and of value. So by a series of considerations analagous to those which we use in other realms the conclusion is reached that there must exist a personal God, in some sense like us, though infinitely greater, who is responsible for this universe in which we live, and with whom, therefore, we may have direct relations in our daily lives.

The technical form in which these arguments have often been stated and the academic titles by which they are named makes it easy to overlook the fact that they are only the application to the subject-matter of religion of methods of reasoning of which we all make use in daily life. It is possible to restate them in simple language and to show that they attempt to answer questions which even the youngest of us soon find ourselves asking. These questions have to do with the causes which account for the world without any of the meanings which explain the world within.

When examined more closely the arguments fall into two groups, which illustrate respectively the narrower and the broader aspects of the method of reasoning. The first group, which includes the so-called cosmological and teleological arguments, is an example of reasoning in the narrower sense of that term. The premise here is certain observed phenomena in the physical universe and in man and the conclusion drawn is that there must be a personal God to account for them. In the case of the cosmological argument the point of departure is a world in process of change. From this fact it is inferred that there must be a Creative Spirit to account for the change.[2] In the case of the teleological argument the point of departure is a world that lends itself to uses.[3] The conclusion drawn is that there must be a purposing mind to account for the observed adaptation.

The second group, which includes the so-called ontological and moral arguments, is an example of reasoning in the broader sense. The premise in this case is not any quality, or qualities, in the physical universe, but the existence of spiritual ideals in the spirit of man. In the case of the ontological argument the point of departure is the idea of a perfect being, and the conclusion drawn is that such a being must exist. In the case of the moral argument the point of departure is man's sense of duty as revealed in conscience, with its categorical imperative, and the conclusion drawn is that there must be a moral

[2] In the older form of the cosmological argument the creative activity of God was found in a series of separate acts, like the six days of creation. To-day we think of cause in a more comprehensive way, as expressing the whole series of influences which make our world what it is. God's creative activity so conceived would be thought of as functioning through a continuous process such as many biologists conceive evolution to be.

[3] As the eye to sight or the wing to flying. The older apologists like Paley and Butler made large use of mechanistic analogies, thinking of God as a kind of gigantic craftsman who makes specific objects for particular uses. Modern advocates of the teleological argument find their proof of adaptation less in any particular quality or qualities of specific objects than in the way in which they all together co-operate to serve far-reaching ends.

deity who is the source of the imperative and who will guarantee the ultimate triumph of the right.

Stated in this way both the ontological and moral arguments derive their force from the conviction that our judgments of value give us trustworthy knowledge of reality.[4] The major premise of each is the immediate intuition of an ideal—in one case an ideal of perfection, in the other of obligation, which is recognized as valid with an inner certainty which needs no other proof. So understood they do not differ in principle from the intuitions which we have been studying in the previous chapter and the certainty they produce is of the same kind.

This was recognized by Kant, so far as the moral argument was concerned. He contrasted this with the cosmological and teleological arguments, which claim to give us demonstration in the scientific sense, as falling in the sphere of the practical reason. By the practical reason he meant substantially what religious people usually call faith, the certainty that comes

[4] Professor Dewey criticises his philosophical predecessors for the use which they make of this assumption. He does not deny that it is valid as far as it affects the special meanings and values with which man is concerned, but he does not think it legitimate to draw conclusions from our judgments of particular values as to the moral quality of the universe as a whole. In the fact that his predecessors have done this, he sees the error of all preceding philosophy from Plato to Kant. But it is difficult to see on what ground he justifies his criticism. In a philosopher who denies that our experience of value has any contribution to make to our knowledge of the real world, the criticism would be in place. But this is not Professor Dewey's position. He admits the principle which underlies the older philosophical interpretations but arbitrarily limits the extent of its possible application. In this he seems to be abandoning the restrained methods of science for the dogmatism of those he criticises.

through immediate insight. His method differed from that of his predecessors, who had made appeal to faith for their certainty of God, in basing the whole weight of the argument upon the moral judgment of duty and minimizing or ignoring the significance of other ideals such as truth or beauty.

This explains his attitude toward the ontological argument which, as we have seen, is really a different form of the appeal to intuition. Instead of classing it with the moral· argument as a form of the practical reason, he associated it with the cosmological and teleological arguments and, treating it in this way, had little difficulty in showing that considered as a syllogism it involved the fallacy of assuming the conclusion which it professed to establish. It is one thing to have the idea of a most perfect being, quite another to affirm the existence of such a being. There is nothing in logic to show that we have the right to pass from one to the other.

In the case of the other two arguments, those from change and from adaptation, the inference drawn seems to follow more directly from the premises. In both the premise from which we start is certain observed facts which are found partly in the physical universe, partly in man's moral and social life. We are living in a changing world, which in the course of its change lends itself to our uses and serves our purposes. From this the inference is drawn that a cause adequate to account for such a world must exist, namely, a being with purposes like man's and power to bring what he plans to accomplishment.

And to many minds over many centuries this way of establishing God's existence has appealed as not only religiously satisfying but as scientifically legitimate. Even Kant, the most acute of all the critics of the arguments, admitted that the teleological argument at least made a strong appeal and that it deserved to be treated with respect. Yet he argued that when closely analyzed it involved the same kind of fallacy which he detected in the ontological argument, namely, the surreptitious introduction into the conclusion of a factor not contained in the premise. The professed purpose of the argument is to discover a cause adequate to account for the world we see, but the implied assumption is that this cause must at the same time be such as to satisfy the religious longings and needs of man. But this result is possible only as we read into the evidence data which our religious intuitions supply; in other words, as we introduce into our procedure judgments of value of a kind which ordinary scientific reasoning excludes.

The Permanent Significance of the Arguments

We may admit that as long as we confine ourselves to explanation in the narrower sense, the kind of explanation with which alone the exact sciences are concerned, this criticism is legitimate. But we have seen that there is another kind of question which we may ask and another kind of explanation which is possible. When we ask, not what kind of cause we can demonstrate to be necessary to account for the effects we see, but what kind of cause gives us the most ade-

quate and satisfying *explanation* of these effects, the
matter is put in a new light. Here the judgments of
value, which reasoning in the narrower sense rules
out, become essential, indeed we may say determining
factors. When one considers a complicated phenom-
enon like adaptation it is not simply the brute facts
used that are relevant to the conclusion, but the persons who use them, and no explanation that ignores
personal valuation of the facts has dealt adequately
with all the data in the case.

Interpreted in this broader sense the old arguments retain a perennial significance. Whether we
agree with Kant that in spite of their plausibility the
cosmological and teleological arguments involve a
fallacy which more rigorous analysis will uncover, or
with many theistic writers acknowledge their logical
validity within definite limits, the fact remains that
for multitudes of persons the way of approach followed by these arguments is the path which has actually led them to their conviction of the existence of
God. Through the experience of dependence and of
limitation which is forced upon us by the events of
every day we are reminded of the greater forces by
which we are encompassed. Contemplating the ceaseless procession of the years, with the changes which
they bring with them in night and day, summer and
winter, youth and age, life and death, we cannot help
wondering who, or what, is responsible for this endless
variety. Turning to nature in our need of food and
shelter and warmth and light and all the myriad and
ever-growing necessities of man, we find her minister-

ing to our uses and it is natural, one might say almost inevitable, that we should conclude that what lends itself to the service of mind must have had mind for its maker. Granting that we cannot demonstrate the existence of God in this way it is still true that multitudes of highly intelligent people have been convinced that of all possible explanations of the world that can be given that of theism is the most reasonable.

When we turn our attention from the outer world to the inner, the evidence of adaptation grows still more impressive. The spiritual world too has its laws, and these laws disclose themselves to the sensitive spirit. These laws too, like the more familiar laws of the physical sciences, have their basis and their illustrations in nature. The moralist's belief in an objective moral order to which he attributes universal validity is confirmed not only by the discovery of recurrent elements in the differing moral codes to which the peoples have given their allegiance but by the disastrous consequences which have followed their persistent violation. So the artist's belief in an ideal world of beauty of which he is not simply inventor, but revealer, is confirmed by the existence of common objects which through all fluctuations of taste have maintained their appeal to lovers of the beautiful. How better account for the persistence of these ideals of goodness and beauty than by postulating, with the prophets of theistic religion, a supreme personality who realizes in himself, or is realizing through others, the ideals after which all lesser persons are striving.

Professor Streeter has made impressive use of this argument in his suggestive book, *Reality*:[5]

"Nietzsche is right," he tells us, "in hailing [intellectual energy and courage] as creative qualities. . . . The point . . . I urge is that [they] are creative forces in exact proportion to the extent to which they are directed toward unselfish ends; they are destructive, in exact proportion as they are directed toward ends that are self-regarding" (pp. 165). ". . . The supremely characteristic manifestation then of the inward quality of the Infinite Creative Life is that which finds expression in the Will to Good. In other words, Strife can create only if it be the expression of Love" (pp. 173, 174).

Mr. Lippmann too is impressed by the surprising agreement which he finds among ethical teachers of different ages and races as to the principles which determine moral excellence. Speaking of the virtues in the catalogue of the moralists he tells us that "though they have many different names, they correspond to an experience so long and so nearly universal that, when understood, they are seen to contain a deposited wisdom of the race."[1]

Even in the case of Beauty, where of all fields agreement would seem most difficult to attain, there are elements of permanence which are recognized by discerning critics. In the Preface to his *Poems*, Professor Santayana has reminded us what these elements are:

"To say that what was good once is good no longer is to give too much importance to chronology. Æsthetic fashions may change, losing as much beauty at one end as they gain at the other, but innate taste continues to recognize its affinities, however remote, and need never change."[6]

This way of reasoning, while taking its departure from our consciousness of obligation and our intuition of ideal perfection, goes beyond the method of intuition as we have thus far studied it in including an element of inference. It invites us to accept, on rational grounds, that one of several possible alternatives which on the whole seems best to account for the judgments of value given in our immediate experience.[7]

Why Many No Longer Find the Arguments Convincing

In our own day, however, we find many people for whom this way of reasoning has lost its force. It is not that new arguments have been discovered which discredit the old position, but that the emotional attitude has changed so that to many people the old arguments no longer seem convincing. Many different factors have combined to produce this alteration of mood, some of them the result of changes in our view of the physical universe, others of changes in ourselves which are the result of our experience with the universe.

To begin with the changes in our view of the physical universe. These have been so revolutionary

[6] New York, 1928, pp. x, xi.

[7] On this whole subject cf. Sorley, W. R., *Moral Values and the Idea of God* (Gifford Lectures for 1914–15) (Cambridge, 1918), and Brightman, E. S., *Religious Values* (New York, 1925), pp. 63, 64.

that they seem to many persons to discredit altogether the conception of God in which religious people have believed in the past, that is to say, a God in
some true sense like ourselves. If there be a God at
all (and of this many are very doubtful), they believe that he must be a God who can find his place in
the extraordinarily complicated and bewildering universe that modern physics and chemistry are recon-
structing for us through the telescope, the microscope, the spectroscope, and the test-tube; a God who
will be at home in Einstein's universe rather than in
Newton's and fit in with all the extraordinary new
discoveries that Professor Eddington has been picturing for us in his fascinating book, *The Nature of
the Physical World*.[8] Such a God, they tell us, can
bear little resemblance to the Father of whom Jesus
spoke, whose care extends to individual men, or even
to the God of Paley or of Butler, who designed the
world as an artist might model a statue and acts upon it directly from time to time. The bare size of the
modern universe alone would make it impossible for
us to believe in a manlike God.

But there is a second, and in many respects even
more important reason, which makes it hard for many
of our contemporaries to believe in the God of the
older theism, namely, the contrast between the facts
of life and the conditions which we should expect to
find if God were really such a being as religious faith
assumes. Adaptation is all very well, we are told, for
the people who are adapted to the universe, but what

8 Gifford Lectures for 1927 (New York, 1929).

of the great number who are unadapted, the misfits and the failures, the suicides and the insane?

This is no new difficulty. Men have felt it in every age from Job's day to our own. But we have been passing through experiences which have pressed the old difficulty home with redoubled force. We must therefore consider this moral difficulty, as well as the theoretical ones, if we are to estimate correctly what reasoning can do to help us on our way to certainty.

2. Difficulties Raised by Physical Science

Contrast Between the Old World and the New

The first of the theoretical difficulties in the way of believing in the personal God of theism is that which is caused by the contrast between the old world and the new. When we compare the universe in which we are living to-day with the world in which Jesus and the Apostles lived—one may go farther and say, with the world in which Luther and Calvin lived—the contrast is so great that it seems impossible to find any point of contact. Jesus lived in a world that was limited in space and time. The earth was a flat surface, fixed in space, with the firmament above in which the heavenly bodies revolved, while below was Sheol, the land of the dead, to which the spirits of those who had passed away descended at death. It was a world that had had a definite beginning and would have as definite an end. Indeed as late as the seventeenth century a theologian was found who

could date to a year the time of its beginning, even if
he was not able as definitely to predict the date when
it would end.[9] This world, so limited in space and
time, was inhabited by a multitude of spirits, good
and evil, which participated in its affairs in various
ways. They were the cause of many of the misfor-
tunes from which man suffered, notably insanity and
disease. They were also the source of many of his
blessings, such as ample crops, recovery from sickness, and victory in war. Protestants, to be sure, unlike their Catholic fellow-Christians, no longer
thought it right to pray to the good spirits, but they
were acutely conscious of the danger to which they
were exposed from the evil spirits, as the experience
of our New England ancestors at Salem abundantly
proves.

What is there in common between a world like this
and the universe in which we are living to-day, a
world of spaces all but infinite, in which countless
suns move in their orbits at inconceivable speed, while
new suns are forming from nebulæ that light our
heaven with their luminous gases; a world as wonderful in its tiniest components as in its most majestic,
each atom a little solar system with its own sun (the
nucleus) and its own planets (the electrons)? Where
is there room in a world like this, where each event
has its appointed place in a system in which everything that happens is bound together by immutable
laws, for the direct initiative of deity in miracle and
revelation? What more natural than to conclude that

9 Archbishop James Ussher (1581–1656).

the kind of God who would be adequate to account for the world of Jesus and of Calvin is wholly inadequate to account for the world in which we are living to-day?

Danger of Exaggerating the Contrast

Yet it is possible to exaggerate the importance of these changes so far as their practical effects on daily life are concerned. Our *theory* of the universe has changed amazingly, to be sure, changed until our imagination grows dizzy. But it is the same universe as it always was and it is doing for us the same things that it always did. The sun still gives us light and the earth food and the night sleep and the sunrise beauty, and we feel about them in our normal moments just as Abraham felt, and Isaiah, and Jesus. For daily life—all the astronomers in the world to the contrary—the earth is flat and fixed and the sun rises in the East and sets in the West and we set our watches by it. Science has told us some things we did not know about these familiar processes which enable us to use them more effectively and to avoid some of the mistakes which our fathers made. And in addition it has revealed to us a whole set of new worlds of which our fathers knew nothing. But it has not made it any less reasonable to use the old world for the well-tried purposes for which men have always used it. Why may we not find similar continuity in the world of our religious experience?

In a recent collection of essays, dealing with the relation of religion and science, Professor Eddington gives us a graphic picture of the contrast between a physicist's theory of the universe and the practical use which he makes of it:

"The learned physicist and the man in the street were standing together on the threshold about to enter a room.

"The man in the street moved forward without trouble, planted his foot on a solid unyielding plank at rest before him, and entered.

"The physicist was faced with an intricate problem. To make any movement he must shove against the atmosphere, which presses with a force of fourteen pounds on every square inch of his body. He must land on a plank travelling at twenty miles a second round the sun—a fraction of a second earlier or later the plank would be miles away from the chosen spot. He must do this whilst hanging from a round planet head outward into space, and with a wind of ether blowing at no one knows how many miles a second through every interstice of his body. He reflects too that the plank is not what it appears to be—a continuous support for his weight. The plank is mostly emptiness; very sparsely scattered in that emptiness are myriads of electric charges dashing about at great speeds but occupying at any moment less than a billionth part of the volume which the plank seems to fill continuously. It is like stepping on a swarm of flies. Will he not slip through? No, if he makes the venture, he falls for an instant till an electron hits him and gives a boost up again; he falls again, and is knocked upwards by another electron; and so on. The net result is that he neither slips through the swarm nor is bombarded up to the ceiling, but is kept about steady in this shuttle-cock fashion. Or rather, it is not certain but highly probable that he remains steady; and if, unfortunately, he should sink through the floor or hit the ceiling, the occurrence would not be a violation of the laws of nature but a rare coincidence.

"By careful calculation of these and other conditions the physicist may reach a solution of the problem of entering a room; and, if he is fortunate enough to avoid mathematical blunders, he will prove satisfactorily that the feat can be accomplished in the manner already adopted by his ignorant companion. Happily even a learned physicist has usually some sense of proportion; and it is probable that for this occasion he put out of mind scientific truths about astronomical motions, the constitution of planks and the laws of probability, and was content to follow the same crude conception of his task that presented itself to the mind of his unscientific colleague."[10]

Why, Professor Eddington asks, should we not follow the same commonsense method in dealing with the realities of religion? We may explain God differently and yet go to him for the same purposes and get the same results.

For what does it mean to believe in God in the simple practical way in which this belief meets us in actual religion, not the religion that men talk about, or lecture about, or write learned books about, but the religion by which they live? It means to have confidence that there is something, or some one, in the universe like us, though infinitely greater and wiser, in touch with our lives and able and willing to help us if we comply with certain conditions; some one with whom we can work, some one to whom we can look up, some one with whom we can commune, some one from whom we may derive strength. That is what belief in God meant to Jesus, and to St. Paul, and to St. Augustine, and to St. Francis, and to Martin Luther, and to John Wesley, and to Cardinal Newman, and to Phillips Brooks. And the one thing we need to know is whether there is anything in the

[10] Arthur S. Eddington in *Science, Religion and Reality*, ed. Needham (New York, 1925), pp. 189–190. By permission of the Macmillan Company, publishers.

discoveries of modern science that has made it any
less possible and reasonable to believe in the existence
of such a God than it was before.

The Symbolic Character of Language

What then is the real difficulty which our modern
critics find with the older theistic arguments? Reduced to its simplest terms it may be stated thus. The
size of the universe, as modern astronomy has revealed it to us, has increased so greatly as to render
God's participation in its affairs unlikely. The *nature* of the universe as revealed to us by modern
physics and chemistry furnishes no evidence that his
participation is real.

These objections have force against the conception of Eve which the humanists criticize. When God is
thought of as a magnified king, having his home in
some literal heaven, from which he intervenes from
time to time in the affairs of earth in arbitrary and
unpredictable ways, or as a clever craftsman, making
the world as a potter might mold his clay, taking
materials that are in themselves dead and lifeless and
breathing into them the breath of life, only to withdraw the same when in his good pleasure he thinks fit
to do so, we have a conception which it is difficult, one
may say, impossible, to reconcile with the orderly universe of modern physics or the vast spaces of modern
astronomy.

But it is not so that the great masters of religion
have thought of God. Firmly as they were convinced

of God's kinship with man they were not less aware of the infinite distances that separated them, distances not in the physical sense merely but in all that concerned nature and ideal. The words in which they described God were words like infinite, eternal, incomprehensible, everlasting, and the mood in which they approached him was the same mood of reverent awe which is characteristic of the greatest of contemporary scientists.

One reason why we find it hard to adjust ourselves to the transition through which we are passing is that we find it so difficult to keep in mind the limitations of language. The words that we use to describe the realities of religion are necessarily symbolic. They are not literal descriptions of those realities—how can they be when these are known to us only in part by immediate experience? They are signs that point us in the direction where experience is to be had. When we speak of God as Creator or as King, that does not mean that we think of him as a human craftsman or as an earthly monarch, only on a vastly larger scale. It means rather that there are aspects of our experience with God which suggest qualities analagous to those which we find in his human prototypes,—qualities like the capacity for initiative or the power of control. Because we still use the old words to describe our present experience it does not necessarily mean that we carry over into our conception of God all the elements which our predecessors took over from the science of their day. And conversely, because we find the old words misleading and

prefer to substitute new symbols for the old it does
not follow that the reality to which they point has
changed, or even that our relations to that reality
have radically altered. It may mean simply that we
have discovered new aspects of that reality which the
old words alone do not adequately express and so
need new words (either as substitutes or as supplements) to denote what that reality has come to mean
to us.[11]

The difficulty is that the words we use are not simple counters in a game of wits. They have emotional quality as well. They carry over from the past
the memory of moods of feeling as well as of moments
of insight. They remind us of hours of worship and
of hours of consecration. And so the proposal to substitute a new word for an old, even though it spring
from no lack of faith in the reality believed in but
only from the desire to express that faith in a less

[11] Professor Streeter, in the work already referred to (*Reality*,
London, 1926), calls attention to the fact that the mechanistic
language used by the physical sciences to describe the phenomena
they study is only a form of metaphor, not less, but more, anthro-
pomorphic than the metaphor of personality used by theists to
describe God, since we know mechanics only through personal
experience as a device used by men to attain their ends:

"Theism pictures the Power behind the Universe as in some way
resembling human personality; this is decried as anthropomorphism, *i. e.*, as a making of God in the image of man. Materialism pictures the Universe as an Infinite Machine; this by analogy may be called mechanomorphism.

"Mechanomorphism is essentially myth; but the dazzling triumphs of machinery in the nineteenth century made it imagina-
tively an attractive myth. Yet every machine is an instrument designed to effect a definitely realized purpose, and is itself the expression of the concentrated intelligence of an inventor. It is fal-
lacious to overlook this, and then apply the metaphor of a machine to the Universe as if the oversight made no difference"
(p. 2).

misleading and ambiguous way, seems to many people to savor of impiety, while to others whose emotional history has been different its retention seems to involve an intellectual dishonesty which is morally reprehensible.

Both of these misconceptions can be illustrated in connection with belief in God. I knew a highly cultivated man, a professor in an important university and a leader in many movements of philanthropy and social reform, who once told me that he could never use the word "father" to designate God because of the unhappy associations which the word called up concerning his own childhood. There are human fathers who are ruthless to their children and there are others who are weakly sentimental. Where this is the case, the emotional states which are appropriate to such relationships become attached to the word and its primary meanings of dependence, kinship, and sympathy are obscured.

We find a similar ambiguity in the word "man," a term which many humanists would substitute for God as the most appropriate symbol of the divine. The man humanists would have us worship is not man as he is to-day but man as he may become, man such as they believe he is capable of becoming. In this personification of the highest human ideal Christians may recognize something analagous to what they themselves mean when they speak of the Holy Spirit. But to most people the word man has just the opposite association. It means "man" as we meet him to-day in all his cruelty, selfishness, and ignorance.

To worship such an object seems to them little short of blasphemous.

It is important, therefore, when we use the word "God," to free ourselves as far as possible from the early emotional associations that gather about the word and to consider the issues raised by modern science in as objective and impartial a fashion as possible.

The Difficulty of Magnitude

Let us take the difficulty of magnitude. This is a difficulty which appeals to our mathematically minded age. Goldwin Smith phrased it a generation ago in words which reflect the conditions of his time:

"The theological geocentricism, which makes our planet the centre of all interest, the especial care of the Divinity, and the sole field of divine action, appears in the Johannine doctrine of the Trinity. It might be possible to imagine Deity stooping from a limited heaven to redeem the inhabitants of earth. It would have been hardly possible to imagine a Being who fills eternity and infinity becoming, for the redemption of one speck in the universe, an embryo in the womb of a Jewish maiden."[12]

But the world of Goldwin Smith was a tiny world compared with the unimaginable distances which are pictured to us in the works of Professor Eddington and of Professor Jeans.

Professor Jeans has tried to give us some idea of the magnitude of these distances by a model drawn to scale. Representing the distances traversed by the earth in its orbit around the sun by a pinhead one-

[12] *Guesses at the Riddle of Existence* (New York, 1898), pp. 165, 166.

sixteenth of an inch in diameter, he computes that on this scale "the nearest star in the sky, Proxima Centauri, must be placed about 225 yards away, and to contain even the hundred stars nearest to our sun in space, the model must be a mile high, a mile long and a mile wide."

But this is only the beginning:

"With our earth's long yearly journey round the sun as a pinhead the whole galactic system" (i. e., the system that contains the family of stars to which our own sun belongs) "is about the size of the American continent. It may be well to pause and try to visualize the relative sizes of a pinhead and of the American continent, before we go on with our mental model-building.

"After we have finished the galactic system, we must travel about 30,000 miles before we begin to set up the next bit of our model, at any rate if we are keeping it to scale. At this distance we place the next family of stars, a family which is probably substantially smaller and more compact than our own galactic family, but is comparable with it both in size and in numbers. So we go on building our model—a family of thousands of millions of stars every 30,000 miles or so—until we have two million such families. The model now stretches for about four million miles in every direction. This represents as far as we can see into space with a telescope; we can imagine the model going on, although we know not how nor where—all we know is that the part so far built represents only a fraction of the universe."[13]

Was it really, one wonders, so much easier for Isaiah or for St. Paul to believe in a God who concerned himself with man? Measured by astronomical miles their heavens were immeasurably nearer than

[13] Jeans, Sir James, *The Universe Around Us* (New York, 1929), pp. 82, 83. By permission of the Macmillan Company, publishers.

ours and their stars incredibly fewer. But to their imagination the heavens were no less vast and the stars as the sands of the seashore for multitude. It was not because the world seemed small that the Psalmist felt that there must be a God but because it was so unbelievably great. "When I consider thy heavens, the work of thy fingers, the sun and the moon that thou hast ordained, what is man that thou art mindful of him and the son of man that thou visitest him?"[14]

The truth would seem to be that in reacting against one form of anthropomorphism our modern critics are in danger of falling into another. Because their imagination staggers at so vast a universe they imagine that a God who could order its destinies would have no interest or energy left to give to such an insignificant creature as man. And even as they voice their doubts the botanist invites us to look with him into the microscope and see the evidence of perfection in the workmanship of even the tiniest constituent of leaf and flower. A God as great as the God of modern science must be is too great to be bounded by the limits of man's imagination.[15]

If indeed it were assumed that man was the only object of God's care, that all this vast universe of ours was created for the sole purpose of ministry to his needs, one might indeed begin to doubt. But this

[14] Psalms 8:4.
[15] Yet one recalls the answer made by a contemporary teacher to a friend who remarked sorrowfully that the vast spaces of modern astronomy had made it impossible any longer to believe in God: "But man is the astronomer."

has never been the faith of the great masters of religion. One of the greatest of the Christian fathers[16] believed that our world was but one of a series of worlds in which the divine Wisdom was unfolding his purpose, and more orthodox and less adventurous thinkers still find room in God's universe for other spirits than man and other purposes than man's salvation.

The Difficulty of Determinism

More real is the second difficulty, that which grows out of the conception of nature held by many scientists. To modern science our universe seems to leave no place for human freedom. It is a universe of law, by which is meant a world in which antecedent follows consequent in invariable succession. It is the function of science to discover the true relation between antecedent and consequent so that it may furnish us with a formula which makes prediction possible. Whatever cannot be brought under the law of orderly succession falls outside the scope of science as scientists understand that scope. What place, we are asked, is there in a world like this for the God of theism, who fulfils his purposes by personal choice and can at any moment initiate a new series of occurrences which have no other antecedent than his own divine will?

This, too, is no new difficulty. We sometimes speak of determinism as if it were a modern invention and of law as if it were inconsistent with divine sov-

[16] Origen (182–251).

ereignty. That was not the view of the Reformers, or for that matter of the mediæval thinkers who preceded them. They too believed in a universe of law; but they saw in law the expression of the divine will. Indeed the fact of law, physical as well as moral, was the major premise of the older theists, the starting point from which they rose to their belief in a moral order of the universe.

In our own day the difficulty has been greatly accentuated by the extension of the scientific postulate of law to the inner life of man. Psychology as at present taught in our universities regards itself as a natural science, like physics or biology, and has taken over the assumptions of natural science. It assumes that every mental state has its antecedents which, could they be completely known, would enable us to predict its consequences with infallible accuracy. And while different schools of psychologists differ in their explanation of the genesis of consciousness they agree in treating it as only the latest chapter in a natural history that began with the dawn of time.

Yet here, too, it is possible to exaggerate the extent of the contrast. Determinism in psychology is no new thing. John Calvin believed in it for all men except the first, and in this, as we have seen, he was only following older masters. Yet Calvin found the acceptance of determinism no bar to belief in moral responsibility, and the men who were drilled in his school possessed a power of initiative that made them leaders in church and state. Here again it may prove that what modern science has done is not to give us a new theory of the will but to buttress an old theory with new arguments.

It is quite true that in addition to the world of law our fathers believed in another world, in which new beginnings took place which were the direct result of the divine initiative. But this belief did not mean that they excluded law from the realm of the divine activity or questioned the fact that through the study of its uniform processes we could gain valid information concerning the nature and purposes of God.

We must remember that though our theories change the facts remain the same. Still in our world of law new beginnings take place, new factors emerge, new choices are made. Life appears. Species succeed one another. Consciousness is born. Great men arise and initiate great epochs. Prophets appear and found new religions. Jesus is born in a tiny province of the Roman Empire and is acclaimed by multitudes as God's chosen Messiah. These are none the less facts because our theories about them have changed. However we may define the uniformity of nature it must be in ways that do not rule these facts out.

Thus it appears that, great as have been the changes in our view of the universe, they are not such as to preclude faith in a God who reveals himself, even though our conception of the manner of his revelation has altered and our view of the range of his activity has enormously increased.

3. How Science Helps Us to Meet the Difficulties It Raises

The Growing Recognition of Unity

But we should be unjust to the analysis which we have been making together if we represented its results as purely negative or permissive. There are many things about the new universe which modern physics is revealing to us which make it *easier* and not harder to believe in a God who can make a difference in human life.

For one thing we have a clearer conception of the unity of the world than our fathers had. They divided the world into two parts, sharply contrasted: nature and the supernatural. Nature was the scene of order and permanence, with uniform laws and unchanging processes. The supernatural was the realm of personality and freedom, where new things came to pass and no one could set bounds to the possible. Science was concerned with nature and worked through reason. Religion had to do with the supernatural and gained its knowledge through revelation.

We see to-day that no such hard and fast line can be drawn. Nature and the supernatural—or to put it in more familiar and less misleading language, the realm of law and the realm of freedom—are not two independent worlds. Rather are they two contrasted aspects of the one undivided world in which we live, and we cannot do justice to all the facts unless we take them both in.

Admitting this fact, however, it makes all the difference in the world where we place our major emphasis, whether we start from the side of uniformity and explain change by that or from the side of freedom and interpret law by that.

A generation ago the first method was in vogue. Materialism was the dominant philosophy of men of science. Personality was not denied but it was explained as a complicated combination of elements that could all be reduced to material particles. Freedom was an illusion, our judgments of value were regarded as the negligible by-product of a cosmic process completely explicable without them. This way of explaining the world still lives on in some forms of contemporary behavioristic psychology.

But scientists as a whole have moved beyond this narrow point of view. We see to-day that if we are to reduce everything to a single principle it is just as easy to start with mind as with matter. From whatever source they may come, this is a world which most thinkers will admit contains meanings and values. And if the world be one world, it is difficult to see how meanings and values can have come to pass in us if they were not first present in the universe that produced us.

The Growing Appreciation of Value

One of the distinguishing features of much of the scientific writing of our day is the recognition that any comprehensive view of the universe must make a generous use of the concept of value. Indeed a writer as judicious as Whitehead finds value an essential element in the constitution of the universe as a whole, present in the electron as truly as in the mind, though in a different way. "Each occasion," he tells us, "in its character of being a finished creature, is a value of some definite specific sort. Thus a mind must be a route whose various occasions exhibit some community of type of value. And the same must be true of "a bit of matter—or an electron."[17] Defining God as "the actual but non-temporal entity whereby the indetermination of mere creativity is transmuted into a determinate freedom," he concludes that God is one of the formative elements in the actual world, which science, if it is to be true to the facts, must recognize.[18]

It is true that some writers, like Bertrand Russell,[19] still believe that as far as purpose is concerned one can draw a hard and fast line between nature and personality and deny to nature any consciousness or plan, while they attribute both to the child whom this blind mother has brought to birth. But to the extent that we make earnest with the unity of the world it becomes increasingly difficult to maintain this dualistic position. There are qualities in nature, as the humanist conceives it, which make natural a form of cosmic worship even for those who discover in the universe no companion so like themselves that he can be

[17] *Religion in the Making* (New York, 1926), p. 109.
[18] *Ibid.*, p. 90.
[19] *Education and the Good Life* (New York, 1926).

rightly described as personal. As man comes to understand nature better and learns to subordinate his individual desires to its orderly ways he finds that it lends itself to spiritual meanings and uses. He finds nature teaching him lessons of beauty, as it has taught the great artists of all generations. He finds it calling forth in him feelings of wonder, as it has called forth such feelings in the great mystics of all the religions. Through the demand that it makes upon him for disinterested service he finds it becoming his most effective teacher in the school of love. So starting at a place far removed from the conclusions of any of the historic religions he may come at last,[1] like Walter Lippmann, to a point where humanistic morals join hands with high religion as it has been interpreted to us by the great teachers of the past. Is it too much to see in this attempt to find a cosmic basis for human virtue a first step along the road which in other ages has led man past nature to God?

No doubt it is impossible for us to conceive what kind of a consciousness God can have. But it may fairly be asked what kind of a God would he be whose consciousness it was possible for us to conceive? We are dealing here with something so stupendous and unimaginable that all our words are only symbols that suggest some particular aspect of a reality which in its completeness is beyond our grasp. Is it any easier to conceive of the four-dimensional universe of modern mathematics than of the infinite consciousness of historic theology? If our inability to picture

[1] *Op. cit.,* pp. 194–200.

the one is no reason for doubting its existence, why should a similar inability be any greater reason for doubting the other?

The New Admission of Mobility

But it is not only in its conception of the unity of the universe that modern science helps us, but also in its conception of its mobility. I know I am entering here on a difficult field for the layman and must tread softly. But this at least we may say with confidence, that whatever else may be true of the universe of modern science, it is not a dead universe. We hear people sometimes speaking of dead matter. But if matter be dead, what, it may be asked, can life be? In the atom, as modern physics pictures it, electric particles are moving about with inconceivable rapidity, following orbits so irregular and unpredictable as to lead some schools of physicists to endow them with a power of initiative suspiciously like the freedom we like to claim for persons. One would be foolish indeed to base his faith in a free and personal God upon the changing theories of a science as mobile as the science of physics. At least this can be said, that in our modern world belief in a Creative Spirit who is bringing new things to pass is not harder but easier.

This is indeed the conclusion which is drawn by an evolutionist like Lloyd Morgan. Surveying the steps by which the various forms of life have succeeded one another upon our planet he finds that the uniformity of the series is broken by the appearance of genuinely new types, types for which apparently we find no adequate preparation in the antecedents which science can discover for us. Comparing the possible ways of accounting for this process of emergent evolution he finds the most reasonable explanation to be that which the theists of all ages have given, namely, the creative activity of a personal God. We cannot indeed demonstrate the existence of such a God, but accepting the data as given to us by natural piety he finds this the most reasonable of all possible explanations.[20]

What Reasoning Can Do for Us and What It Cannot Do

But when all has been said, we are still moving in the field of theory and of possibility. Probability is balanced against probability, with the scale inclining now on this side, now on that. Certainty still eludes us.

On the face of it this seems a discouraging situation until we remember what are the conditions under which reason operates. In the nature of the case it can give us demonstrative proof only in the case of objects from which the personal equation has been excluded. But in religion, as we have seen, the personal equation is an essential element in the proof. What reasoning can do for us is not to provide a sub-

---

[20] Morgan, C. L., *Emergent Evolution* (Gifford Lectures for 1922), (New York, 1927). *Cf.* also Smuts, J. C., *Holism and Evolution* (New York, 1926).

stitute for our first-hand appreciation of values but to criticize our definition of the objects to which the values attach. Its function is not so much proof as the redefinition which makes conviction possible, and it fulfils its function not when it demonstrates God for us but when it shows that the belief in God which we hold is consistent with all the other data in our known world.

We should be on our guard, therefore, against identifying our faith in God with the acceptance of current scientific theories, even if those theories seem to fit in with the contentions of traditional theism. What the science of one age has proved the science of another may lead us to question. If our faith is to rest on a foundation that cannot be shaken we must dig deeper and find our evidence in first-hand religious experience.

More important, therefore, for our present purposes than the theoretical argument on one side or the other is the practical attitude which our men of science are taking toward the questions of religion. It is an interesting fact that among our students of physical science—mathematicians, astronomers, physicists, biologists—many of the most eminent are themselves believers in God, and this not simply in the theoretical and academic sense in which we have been talking about belief thus far but in the sense in which religious people have always believed in God, as a practical and helpful influence in their own lives.

One has only to think of such men as Whitehead

among mathematicians, Millikan and Pupin among physicists, Eddington among astronomers, and Lloyd Morgan and Thompson among biologists, to recall the fact that those who still believe in a God who makes a difference for life find themselves in good company.[21]

I am well aware that this fact of itself cannot act as a substitute for our own personal belief or relieve us of the responsibility for considering the evidence for ourselves. But it does at least this for us, that it removes the adverse presupposition. It increases the number of witnesses for the defense. So far as the argument from authority has any weight at all, it is reinforced by these new and more recent witnesses.

4. THE DIFFICULTY PRESENTED BY THE FACT OF EVIL

The Difficulty Stated

If there is nothing in the results of modern science which makes it impossible to believe in the God of religion, while there is much that helps to make such a

---

[21] Professor Wieman's criticism of the tendency of some apologists to seize "on the pronouncements of some famous scientist when he speaks about matters outside his specialty, especially about religion, and to hold up his pious statements as evidence for the truth of religious belief" (*Christian Century*, December 18, 1929, p. 1572), is quite in place when the scientist in question claims knowledge in technical matters connected with the science of religion. But on two points the evidence of such a scientist is not only relevant but important—one, as to the reality of his own religious experience; the second, that in the field of his own specialty he has found nothing which has made religious conviction intellectually untenable to him.

faith credible, why do we find so many able and sincere men still unconvinced? This brings us to the second of the difficulties already referred to, that which grows out of the contrast between the facts of life and what we should expect to find if the God in whom we profess to believe were real.

Here we reach the most profound of our difficulties, that which grows out of the presence of evil in the world. One may admit that there is much in our world that seems to suggest meaning and value, but this should not blind our eyes to the facts which seem to point in an opposite direction. Nature is the kindly nurse; she is also the ruthless destroyer. The sun that warms the earth also parches it; the rain that fertilizes the soil may become a devastating torrent. The same forces that produced man have put within him passions that threaten to destroy him; the world that gave us a Jesus has given us a Nero. One cannot take the good and ignore the evil. One cannot reason from a normally functioning life to a beneficent Creator, and pass over the heartbreak and the tragedy of less normal lives. If we are to go to logic for our God, is it not more reasonable to believe in a God who is morally indifferent or who, if good, is unable to bring his will to prevail; in a finite God (such as H. G. Wells has pictured[23]) who is doing his best to surmount obstacles which may prove insuperable unless we come to his aid. Unless we can find meaning in the darkest side of life as well as in the brightest we can never attain certainty.

[23] *God the Invisible King* (New York, 1917).

*How the Philosophers Have Dealt with the Problem
of Evil*

Ever since philosophy began philosophers have
been wrestling with this difficulty and they have
found much that is helpful to say. Some things that
they have said find ready confirmation in familiar
human experiences; as, for example, the fact that
much suffering is the result of the misuse of human
freedom; and that, even when this is not the case, and
the misfortune that befalls appears arbitrary and
undeserved, it will be seen on closer inspection to be
the result of the operation of universal laws, the effect of which is on the whole beneficent. But for the
most part they have concerned themselves with more
ultimate questions, such as why evil is here at all, and
what uses it serves.

Their explanations have varied from the frank acceptance of evil as an independent principle in the universe which the good God may oppose and in a measure
control, but which he cannot completely destroy, to
the view which sees in evil only good out of its setting.
Plato and his successors have on the whole preferred
the former solution. Pantheists of all schools, from the
Stoics to Hegel, have inclined to the latter. Christian
Science, with its assurance that all disease is illusion,
illustrates one form of the pantheistic solution.

The explanation which has seemed most satisfying,
especially since the general acceptance of the theory
of evolution, has been the view which accounts for
evil as a necessary element in progress. Pain, for ex-

ample, is here because it has lessons to teach which we could not learn without suffering. Sin is here because it is an inevitable incident in a world where free personalities are being trained in character.

There is much in what we know of the structure of the universe which makes this explanation credible. When pain is thought of as something arbitrary and adventitious, which God can send or withhold at his good pleasure,[24] its occurrence in the particular form in which it meets us in human life presents an all but insoluble problem. But we know to-day that pain is not something that exists in and of itself, but is the necessary accompaniment of certain nervous and mental states that pass imperceptibly through indifference into pleasure.[25] As such, pain fulfils an economy in our life which we now see to be indispensable. It teaches us some of our most important lessons. It is the condition of some of our keenest enjoyments. It warns us against danger; it opens the door to sympathy, and in a hundred ways performs useful functions in the economy of our life. If only we could regulate and control it better; if only its useful functions were not accompanied by so many that seem harmful, it would present no insuperable difficulty.

In the darker problems of moral evil also the conception of discipline has some help to give. Freedom, as far as we can see, is essential to the full development of character and freedom carries with it the possibility of wrongdoing with all its disastrous con-

[24] *Cf.* Hall, C. C., *Does God Send Trouble?* (New York, 1895).
[25] *Cf.* Marshall, Henry Rutgers, *Pain, Pleasure, and Æsthetics* (London, 1894).

sequences. It takes more to make a man than to make a clock. To make a good clock, all that you need to do is to make a good machine. But man is free personality, with all that this implies. In a world meant to train men, pain and sin and failure can be regarded as the raw material of character. Paul became a greater spirit because of his stripes and of his imprisonments, Milton because of his blindness, Lincoln because of that which gave him his sad face and seared brow.

Where the Solution of Philosophy Is Inadequate

But to say this leaves unaccounted for the great mass of evil in the world which appears to be the product of pure chance or which apparently issues in no compensating good. If pain always taught its appropriate lesson or sin were always followed by repentance, we might find moral compensation for suffering. But, alas, it is not so. There is so much in life that seems wanton and fickle, suffering that only hardens and embitters, moral lapses that are followed by no corresponding refining of character, tragedies that defy reason and outrage our sense of justice. So far as we can look into the future there seems no reason to expect that a time will ever come when such areas of inexplicable evil will not remain. If what we now see of nature's dealings with man is all there is to be known, no solution seems possible.

We may thank the humanists for reminding us that much of the evil in the world is preventable evil and for calling upon us to use the help which science can give in removing the causes which have produced it. The fact remains that when all has been done that science can do there still remain these vast areas of misery, heartbreak, and tragedy, which it is not in our human power to alter or to remove.

What can we do in view of facts like this? Must we take them as we find them, solacing ourselves with such insight as science may be able to give us into the causes which have produced them; or may we believe that a wiser mind than ours is concerned with them, and a stronger will is at work which can overrule them for good?

That there is in fact such a wise mind at work and such a strong will has been the faith of theistic religion in the past and is still its faith to-day; a faith which, like the humanist faith with which we have contrasted it, appeals to the future for its justification. Just because we are dealing with a world still unfinished, a process still incomplete, we are not limited to the evidence which is already at hand. New evidence is being created all the time and in the production of this new evidence we ourselves may have a part to play. This brings us to the last of our four pathways to certainty, the way of experiment.

CHAPTER VI

THE WAY OF EXPERIMENT: OR THE PRACTICE OF THE PRESENCE OF GOD

1. The Contribution of Experiment to Certainty.

The Way of Experiment—Why Experiment Is Necessary in Religion—How Experiment Is Possible in Religion.

2. The Use of Hypothesis in Experiment.

The Place of Hypothesis in Scientific Experiment—The Sense in Which God Is Hypothesis for the Religious Man—The Permanent and the Variable in the Religious Hypothesis—The Christian Form of the Religious Hypothesis.

3. The Religious Life as the Progressive Verification of the Religious Hypothesis.

How the Verification of Religion Differs from the Verification of Science—The Religious Life as a Way of Validating Faith in God—Worship and Service as Parallel Forms of the Test by Experiment—Christian Missions as a Way of Checking the Individual Test by Co-operative Experiment.

4. The Christian Way of Dealing with Evil.

Two Ways of Dealing with Evil—Jesus as an Example of the Christian Way of Dealing with Evil—How Prayer Helps Us to Master Evil—How Prayer Bears Fruit in Love—The Social Gospel as the Rethinking of the Religious Ideal of Love in the Light of Modern Science—The Practicability of the Christian Ideal for Society.

The way of experiment differs from the other three ways we have been considering, partly in its active character, partly in its continuing character. In experiment we participate in a test which is still going on.

The reason why religious people need to test their beliefs by experiment is because we are living in a world which is still in the making. This is true both of the life of the individual and of society. We win our certainty of the reality of God by practising his presence in our own lives. We confirm and clarify this certainty by co-operating with others of like mind in proving that the life he makes possible in us is possible also in society. The form of the test is the life of prayer as consummated in the life of love. Through prayer we enter into conscious relations with God, who is not only supreme ideal but ultimate reality and by drawing upon his resources of goodness, of wisdom, and of power, gain the courage and inspiration we need to meet the strain of life in the spirit of love. The test we make in our own individual life is confirmed by the experience of those who have made the same test before or with us. What God may have in store for the future must be determined by the experiments of those who come after us. In defining the condition of these experiments we need to learn all that science can teach us. In the meantime we must live by the light we have, realizing that the farther we can extend the area of our present certainty the firmer foundation we shall be laying for the fuller knowledge of the generations that will succeed us.

1. The Contribution of Experiment to Certainty

The Way of Experiment

We have considered in turn the three most familiar methods of winning certainty in religion: the way of authority, the way of intuition, the way of reasoning. One more remains—in some respects the most significant of all—the way of experiment.

The way of experiment differs from the other three methods which we have considered in that when we experiment we are not content to base our confidence on what has already happened, whether this happening has taken place in nature, in our own lives, or in the lives of others. We turn our faces to the future and anticipate results still to be attained. More than this, we ourselves contribute to the coming of these results. We not only contemplate what God has done for others in the past; we practise his presence in our own lives.

The way of experiment differs from the way of authority in its active character. When we experiment we are not simply spectators but participants in the test. We analyze our problem into its component parts and when we have found the elements that are relevant to the test we wish to make we devise conditions which will make their isolation possible so that we may tell whether they are or are not responsible for the result that follows.

The way of experiment differs from the way of intuition in its continuing character. In intuition the truth comes to us once for all in a flash of insight. But it comes often in an inadequate and misleading setting, and in our subsequent reflection form and substance tend to be confused and our subjective imagining to take the place of objective reality. In experiment we translate our insight from faith into practice. We put it to work and see whether it will do what it promises.

The method of experiment supplements the way of reasoning by increasing the data with which reason can deal. In our ordinary reasoning we make inferences from data already at hand. When we experiment we appeal from the past and the present to the future, that we may gain new materials for further inference.

There is a further respect in which the method of experiment differs from all three of the other ways of reaching certainty. Authority, intuition, and reasoning, each in its own way, define for us the convictions that we wish to test. Experiment is our way of verifying the accuracy of the definition. So far as the test is successful we continue to make use of our hypothesis in its present form, but when, as often happens, our experiment brings to light new data of which our statement has taken no account we revise it so that it may be retested by further experiment.

Yet while for convenience we have contrasted experiment as an independent method with the other three, it is clear that this is true only in part. In fact, as we shall see, all four methods are parts of a single method, and we reach assured results only through a combination of them all. Authority conserves for us the results of past experiment. Intuition enables us to recognize the significance of present experiment. Reasoning defines the condition under which all valid experiment must be conducted and draws appropriate inferences as to its results. We have not taken leave of any one of the three when we have turned to the others.

Why Experiment Is Necessary in Religion

In the physical sciences the use of experiment as a test of truth is universal. Indeed, we may say that science in the sense in which we moderns use the term began when men began to make earnest with experiment. Progress in science is conditioned upon the scientist's ability to devise a technique which will make possible effective experiment or, in other words, which will make it possible to isolate all the elements that are irrelevant in any particular case in order to concentrate attention upon the one issue that matters.

In questions that concern the relation between persons such complete isolation is impossible. Here we are dealing with conditions so complex that anything like mathematical demonstration is out of the question. Nevertheless, as far as progress in human affairs is possible at all, it takes place through experiment. We try different methods and retain the one that proves in experience the best. We compare different forms of government—democracy, aristocracy, monarchy—as they have been actually practised by men, and draw our conclusions accordingly. We try out different schemes of social betterment or watch others trying them—socialism, communism, single tax, profit-sharing, the co-operative movement, as the case may be—in order to discover how far each achieves the result it promises, or, if it fail, where it fails and why. Many a Utopia that reads well in the library breaks down when you come to put it into practice because of the frailty of the human instruments who must put it into execution. To run Plato's republic you must have Plato, and not Plato only, but citizens who are willing to live under his government.

The claims of religion must submit to a similar test. So far as religious faith has to do with the future its anticipations must be justified by the event. This is true of those anticipations which concern the future of the individual. It is even more true of predictions which forecast the relations of men in society.

The reason why religious people need to test their beliefs by experiment is because religion is concerned with a world which is still in the making. It is not enough for us to know that God did such and such things in the past, or even that he is doing such and such things to-day. We wish to be assured that he will continue to do so, and that he will do so over constantly increasing areas and in lives that now seem untouched by his presence. For only so can our confidence in his power to master the evil in the world be justified.

How Experiment Is Possible in Religion

Our inability, in the case of persons, to secure the complete isolation of the factors under investigation, which is the aim of the physical sciences, is sometimes cited as a proof that useful experiment is impracticable in personal relationships.[1] Those who take this view overlook the fact that for our knowledge of truth it is just as important that we should study the operation of wholes as of their parts. It is not enough to study eye and ear and brain. We must learn how all together combine to make the growing active, functioning thing we call the body. Nor is it enough to study the individual, whether it be a plant, an animal, or a man. We must learn how the action of the individual is modified by its environment. And this is possible only as we study large numbers of individuals as they are living their lives under normal conditions.

If this is true of living creatures in general, how much more is it true of man, who is not only a part of the physical universe but self-conscious personality, with ideals, convictions, and purposes. To learn what man is like we must not only take him apart and analyze his component parts in the laboratory and the dissecting room. We must watch him at his work and at his play; in his home, in his office, and at his prayers; doing the things, thinking the thoughts and experiencing the emotions which are natural to man when he is unaware that any one is watching him.

[1] *Cf.* Burtt, E. A., *Principles and Problems of Right Thinking* (New York, 1928), p. 447.

It is not only desirable to do this. It is possible to do so under conditions which approximate the requirements of scientific experiment. For in the case of conscious beings, like persons, it is often possible by the active co-operation of the will to secure the modification of action which is necessary for a true experiment.

If this were not so, the progress that has been made in our knowledge of the laws of hygiene would have been impossible. This progress has been brought about not only through the controlled experiments of the laboratory and of the dissecting room but by the observation of multitudes of ordinary people under the conditions of their daily life. It has been greatly assisted by the co-operation of a selected group who, without leaving their homes or their business, have been willing to modify their habits for the purpose of assisting in the experiment. While we have not been able by such methods to secure exact knowledge of what will happen in every case, we have gained a large enough body of data to justify our confidence in many measures of large social consequence.[2]

This reference to hygiene suggests the kind of experiment which is needed in religion. It is the kind which is practicable for normal people under the conditions of their daily life. In religion, as in medicine, pathology has its place, and much may be

[2] Vaccination is a case in point. The question whether the reasons which justify the practice are adequate must be determined by comparing the results which follow in those social groups which use the practice with those that follow in the groups that do not.

learned from the studies now being carried on by our psychiatrists as to the causes of mental and moral abnormality. But it is possible to overdo the pathological. In religion, as in medicine, health is normal, not disease. When Horace Bushnell, in his *Christian Nurture*,[3] enunciated the principle that it is the natural thing for a child brought up in a Christian family to grow up a Christian, he took an important forward step in our understanding of the religious life.

In the most general sense of that term we may regard all human history as an experiment in applied religion. When we study history we discover the part that religion has played in the life of man. We assist at the birth of the great religions, follow their growth, and in some cases their decay, and note the effects which they have produced upon the life of their adherents. We observe, too, the effects that have followed in periods of religious doubt or dissolution and are enabled to draw general conclusions as to the function which religion fulfils in the life of man and as to the trustworthiness of the accounts that particular religions give of themselves.

Our immediate interest, however, is not in this more general form of social experiment but in its more familiar form as involving the conscious cooperation of the participants. In this narrow and more exact sense experiment has always played a large part in the life of religious people. The great mystics in particular have developed a technique for

[3] Hartford, 1846.

the study of the religious life which has anticipated many of the most significant findings of modern psychology. But quite apart from these exceptional cases there have been in every age a large number of people who have taken their religion seriously and in doing so have changed their previous habits of living in such a way as to afford true, even if incomplete, examples of scientific experiment. And there are many more who might do this if they would. The possibilities of experiment of this kind in religion we have now to explore. Only when we have done this shall we be in a position rightly to estimate the significance of the larger social experiment of which all history is part.

2. The Use of Hypothesis in Experiment

The Place of Hypothesis in Scientific Experiment

There are three conditions to which every successful experiment must conform. It must begin with a hypothesis sufficiently precise to give direction to the experiment and make possible some effective control of its results. It must admit of some form of verification open to the observation of the investigator and capable of being confirmed by the concurrent observation of other competent, impartial persons. It must continue for a long enough period and be repeated a sufficient number of times to eliminate preventable errors.

The function of hypothesis in experiment is to afford a standard by which success or failure can be judged. My hypothesis in any experiment defines the issue I wish to put to the test. Whether I am interested with Laplace in discovering whether planets are formed by the condensation of nebulæ or with Harvey in learning whether the heart is a pump which sets the blood circulating through the veins, I must first state what it is that I wish to determine so clearly that those who join with me in my experiment can understand what we are trying to establish. My statement of the issue to be determined is my hypothesis.

While it is true that a hypothesis is useful according to its definiteness, this does not mean that hypotheses are rigid things which cannot be modified. On the contrary the history of science is the history of the progressive modification of hypotheses to meet the increasing complexity of phenomena as disclosed by experimentation. Ptolemy's hypothesis of a sun that moved around the earth was adequate to account for the facts known to Ptolemy. But Copernicus had to modify it to account for the new facts brought to life by his experiments. And the hypothesis of Copernicus of bodies moving through a motionless space at definite rates of speed has been modified by Einstein for a similar reason. It is the same nature that man studies in each succeeding generation, but with the improvement of his technique he learns more about nature as the centuries pass and the progress of his increasing knowledge is registered in the hypotheses by which he explains nature.

Closely allied with hypotheses in the technical

sense, yet clearly distinguishable from them, are the basic assumptions on which all scientific reasoning rests. These basic assumptions are often called postulates. They are the premises which furnish the point of departure for experiment in any form, necessary not only to the existence of each particular science but of scientific procedure itself.

Among these basic assumptions, necessary, as we have seen, to the existence of science in any form, are such as these: That there is an order of nature which expresses the way in which things may be counted upon to happen; that man has capacity within limits to understand what that order is; and that the scientific method is the way in which trustworthy knowledge of that order is to be gained. These postulates have hypothetical character in that they have never been completely demonstrated. But they differ from hypotheses of the more familiar kind in that they are not subject to doubt. To doubt them would be not to disprove some particular hypothesis but to make the proof or disproof of any hypothesis whatever impossible. They furnish the major premise on which all future argument must rest, a premise most certain just because it is incapable of proof.

Upon the basis of these fundamental postulates the representatives of the different sciences proceed to erect more specific assumptions which define their conception of the universe up to date and form the hypotheses which they attempt either to confirm or to correct by scientific experiment.

An example of hypothesis in this more technical

sense is the modern physicist's theory of radio activity. According to this view the phenomena which the physics of an earlier day attributed to different and independent causes such as gravitation or electricity are believed to be manifestations of particular combinations of elements which are the ultimate constituents of nature as a whole. In like manner, where the older chemistry listed a definite number of entities which were assumed to be the irreducible units of matter we now believe them all to be forms of simpler units which combine with one another in different ways. Chemists have devised mathematical formulæ to define what those ways are. These formulæ are chemical hypotheses and determine the nature of chemical experiment. However high their degree of probability they are necessarily tentative in character and may at any time require correction as a result of further experiment.

But the tentative character which scientists attribute to hypothesis in this sense does not apply to the basic assumptions which furnish the framework of all scientific procedure. Here there can be no question of alternative possibility if science in any form is to continue to exist.

Thus it appears that science makes use of assumptions of two kinds and could not do its work without them: the basic assumptions known as postulates and the provisional assumptions known as hypotheses. Assumptions of the first kind are accepted without question. As postulates universally valid they express the sum of the scientist's certainties. Assumptions of the second kind are held tentatively. They express probable judgments. It is the aim of scientific procedure to make these probable judgments certain by devising hypotheses so accurate that they will meet the test of repeated experiment without the necessity of redefinition.

The Sense in Which God Is Hypothesis for the Religious Man

God is to the religious man both postulate and hypothesis. He is postulate in the sense that he furnishes the fundamental assumption from which all living religion draws its vitality, the assumption that our human values have cosmic roots which make communion with ultimate reality possible. In addition, and more specifically, the religious man makes God his hypothesis in the sense that he regards some one way of conceiving the nature of God as more adequate than other ways, let us say the Christian way as distinct from the Buddhist way or the Mohammedan way, or, within Christianity, some specific way of stating the Christian conception of God as contrasted with some other possible way. Our hypothesis concerning God defines that part of our thought about God which has not yet been completely verified by experiment and which is therefore capable of progressive redefinition. But we would never experiment with God at all if we were not already in possession of certain basic certainties concerning him which we share with all men who are living the religious life.

One of these basic certainties has to do with the source of our moral and spiritual ideals. It may be stated thus : That there is a moral and spiritual order which is no less real than the aspect of reality made known to us through the senses. This corresponds to the scientific postulate of an order of nature which expresses the way in which things may be counted upon to happen. A second assumption has to do with man's capacity to know this ideal order. It is the assumption that the divine, which is also the excellent, has been made known to men in definite and recognizable ways so that we may be sure not only that deity exists but also within limits what it is like. This corresponds to the scientific assumption that it is possible for man, within limits, to know what the order of nature is. A third assumption has to do with the way in which that knowledge is to be gained. It is the assumption— made alike by greatest prophet and by simplest believer—that *a trustworthy knowledge of God is made possible to man by his capacity to act upon his ideals*, so that, when he trusts and follows that which is most excellent, he enters into communion with deity. This corresponds with the scientific assumption that the way to learn of nature's laws is to use the technique of the exact sciences.

On the basis of these fundamental assumptions religious men proceed to erect more detailed hypotheses as to the nature of the ideal order and the way in which it makes its presence known to them. These hypotheses differ from the corresponding hypotheses of science in that they are concerned with a reality which can be known to us completely only through our judgments of value. But in all other respects they must conform to the tests by which hypotheses are judged. As the ultimate source of goodness, beauty, and truth, God's existence cannot be scientifically demonstrated. But this does not mean that there are no tests by which our knowledge of deity can be validated. God is the subject of experiment in religion in the same sense in which nature is the subject of experiment in science. And as the hypotheses of the different sciences sum up our knowledge of nature up to date and define the issues on which further inquiry is necessary, so the doctrines of religion sum up man's experience of God up to date and define the issues on which further experiment is necessary.

It may seem strange to some people to use the word hypothesis to describe the attitude which the worshipper takes to his God. Does not the word carry with it on its face an element of tentativeness which rules out from the start the certainty which is the object of our quest? There are not a few of our contemporaries who believe that it does and see in this fact a merit rather than a defect. They find ethical, as well as intellectual, reasons which make tentativeness inevitable even at this central point of the religious life. How, they ask, can love, which is never happy unless it can share, be content to enjoy its own certainty as long as there is any one left in the world who is still doubtful of God's existence?[4]

[4] *Cf.* Burtt, E. A., *Religion in an Age of Science* (New York, 1929), p. 138: "If my love is sincere, in other words, my attitude must be one of entire tentativeness toward even the noblest ideas and the most appealing emotions that come to me from my own

Such a view fails to distinguish between hypothesis in the narrow sense in which we are using the term here and the basic postulates on which our certainty of God depends. Just because God is known to us only in part, there must always be tentative elements in our thought of him, and the longer we live and the wiser we grow the more we shall be conscious of how much there is about him of which we are still ignorant. But this insight is quite consistent with a confident assurance concerning certain basic verities of which we are not in doubt. Indeed it is because of what we know already that we are sure that there is still more to be known.[5]

When we say then that our knowledge of God is hypothetical we do not mean that we have no certain knowledge of God, or even that we know him only in part. We express our faith that it is possible for us to know him better. Our hypotheses define for us the range of the possible better knowledge which it is our aim by progressive experiment to translate into certainty.[6]

particular religious heritage, for only so can I be entirely ready at any time to appreciate the real nature of the religious puzzles that disturb my neighbor and aid him in attaining the kind of answer that will meet just his difficulties and not those of myself or some other persons who are long since dead.

Cf. also Wieman, H. N., "Wrong Ways to Justify Religion," *Christian Century,* December 18, 1929, p. 1573: "The apologist for religion should present all our most sacred beliefs and programmes of action as tentative and experimental. Until he does that he can never make Christianity acceptable to this age."

[5] "If I did not know thee, I would not seek thee."

[6] *Cf.* Baillie, John, *The Interpretation of Religion* (New York, 1928), pp. 373–380. Professor Baillie's criticism of the use of hypothesis to describe the affirmations of faith is due, at least in part, to his failure to distinguish the two forms of assumption which we have called postulate and hypothesis.

The Permanent and the Variable in the Religious Hypothesis

In defining the religious hypothesis, therefore, as well as the parallel hypotheses of science, it is necessary to distinguish its permanent from its variable elements. In every religious hypothesis, the basic assumptions which form the postulates of all vital religion reappear in some form. Through all the variations which emerge in the course of religious history they persist and their persistence gives vitality and consistency to the religious life. These postulates, as we have seen, have to do with the nature of deity, with our capacity to know God, and with the way in which that knowledge comes. They are the precondition of vital religion in every form. More important than any specific question which may meet us in connection with differing forms of religious faith is the question whether these basic assumptions can maintain their validity.

The first issue to be determined in connection with the religious experiment and the one which is basic to all the rest is as to the trustworthiness of our assumption of an ideal order. Are our dreams of a better and more satisfying life dreams only, or are they rooted in the nature of things so that when we follow the best we know we put ourselves in touch with that which is most real in the universe? That we do so touch reality has been the conviction of the prophets of the great religions. They may conceive the nature of that reality in widely different ways, some picturing it as changeless perfection, existing independently of all contact with our transitory and imperfect world, others as a living personality actively concerned in our affairs as the Creative Spirit helping us to realize in ourselves and in our world an ideal which awaits its full consummation in the future. But that religion brings us into touch with reality, and that of the most basic and enduring kind, all the great religious teachers agree.

In this the teachers of religion are saying only what the philosophers have said before them. But religion goes farther than philosophy. It pictures the divine as revealing itself in history and showing man what the true life is like. Here again the pictures differ widely, some emphasizing active attitudes like consecration and communion, others the more passive virtues of resignation and inwardness. Buddhists believe that man conceives the divine most truly when he suppresses the element of desire and finds his ideal of perfection in the dreamless sleep of Nirvana, whereas the Christian thinks of God as the life-giver, expressed most clearly in the life that reveals itself in the gift of self. But in each case there is a common assumption that man is capable of knowing what God is like.[7]

The difference between religion and philosophy appears most clearly in connection with the third of

[7] It is important to realize that this assumption is found as truly in the mystical religions which describe God as unknowable and indefinable as in the theistic faiths which picture his nature in terms of intellect or will. In each case it is assumed that knowledge of the divine is possible, though the content of that knowledge, and the way in which it is attained, is differently conceived. This is

the three convictions which underly all forms of the religious hypothesis, namely, that it is possible for the individual to-day, through consecration and prayer, to attain a trustworthy knowledge of the divine. Religions differ as to the way in which they conceive that knowledge and the process through which it is attained, some emphasizing the need of renunciation and asceticism, others giving the place of honor to outgoing and creative love. Buddhism follows the first way and Christianity the second, though neither religion has carried its emphasis so far as altogether to exclude the method recommended by the other. But both believe that the way for man to attain knowledge of God is to trust and follow the best that he knows, as God shall help him to see it.

And if all men agreed as to what is best, the tests to be applied in religious experiment would be comparatively simple ones. Since this is not the case, however, the issue to be determined becomes more complicated. It is not simply a matter of testing a single generally accepted hypothesis by repeated experiment. It is rather a case of deciding between different forms of hypothesis by comparing the effects which follow from acting upon each.

Thus it appears that the issue to be tested in the course of the religious experiment is not simply

as true of Buddhism, with its apparently atheistic philosophy, as of Christianity, with its theistic faith. Buddhists believe that when Gautama received enlightenment he gained trustworthy knowledge of ultimate reality, even though the language in which he described that knowledge is wholly negative. We find a similar combination of a positive faith with a negative terminology in many of the great Christian mystics.

whether the religious man's faith in God can be justified in the basic form in which it is shared by all genuinely religious people but also which of the different ways of defining God is most in accord with the facts.

The Christian Form of the Religious Hypothesis

We may illustrate the way in which the religious hypothesis varies by recalling the form in which it appears in Christianity, the religion with which we of the Western world are most familiar. Christianity shares with other religions the fundamental conviction as to the reality of an ideal order with which man can have practical relationships. It differs from them partly in the way this ideal order is conceived, partly in the way in which its presence is made practically effective in the life of man. As to the first, Christians believe that we come closest to understanding what is most excellent in the universe when we observe man in his most unselfish and co-operative attitude, as it is pictured to us in the life, the death, and the continuing influence of Jesus and in the persons who have most closely approximated the type of life which he lived. As to the second, they believe that man achieves his truest and best self when through whole-hearted trust in God, as revealed in self-sacrificing love through Jesus, he receives strength to follow him in his ministry of love. The religious hypothesis, therefore, as formulated by Christians is that God, who is himself love, is calling men to the life of love and through the impartation of his spirit of insight, sympathy, and faith is more and more enabling them to realize it.

In making love central in their thought of God, Christians are not forgetful of the other aspects of the ideal life as they are expressed in such words as truth, beauty, and justice. No attempt to compress so august a conception as that of deity into a single word can hope to succeed. Christians share with the philosophers of all the schools the conception of God as truth. God is the ultimate standard of right thinking to which all human thought must conform and all that science can teach us about the structure of the universe or the working of the human mind must find its place in our thought of him. Christians share with the artists of every age the thought of God as beauty. God is the final harmony in the universe, the ideal norm which gives its meaning and excellence to every combination of form and color, and nothing that art can show us of the way in which these treasures can be made available for the enrichment of the human spirit is without bearing upon our appreciation of him. Christians share with the upright and loyal men of every country the thought of God as justice. God is the principle of order in human society, the basis of our confidence that right will ultimately prevail in the relations of men, and no step that has been taken in man's upward climb from the beast but sheds light on his character and illuminates his purposes. Finally, Christians share with the mystics of all the religions the thought of God as mystery. God is the other side of nature,

after which thought is ever reaching out but to which
it can never attain—the unexplained and the inexplicable—and no mood that stirs man to reverence
and awe, as he contemplates the wonders of the universe, but has its secret source in him. But above and
beyond all this, God is love, the outgoing spirit that
manifests itself in creation and renewal and that has
its most signal manifestations in the Cross of Jesus
Christ.

To Christian faith this God of wisdom, beauty,
justice, mystery, and love is the God of the real
world. He evidences his presence in nature through
the orderly processes by which life is generated, nur-
tured, and enriched. He reveals himself in history
through great men of every race and profession,
through founders and saints of the great religions,
and through the literature and the institutions which
record and mediate the deep spiritual insights won by
leaders of men. He reveals himself most directly
through Jesus, through the Bible, which records the
life of Jesus, and through the church, which carries
on his ministry. He makes his presence felt to-day in
the personal experience of countless individuals whose
recurrent intuitions of the good, the beautiful, and
the true bring meaning and value into life and assure
man of his kinship with the eternal. What God has
done in the past the Christian believes he will continue to do in the future. He anticipates a time when
the obstacles which now limit his activity will be
overcome and both in the individual and in society
love will prove itself to be in fact the greatest thing

in the world. This confidence not only helps him to meet the responsibilities and temptations of his own life with courage and faith; it inspires him to share his faith with others, in the hope that it may do for them what it has done for him.

3. THE RELIGIOUS LIFE AS THE PROGRESSIVE VERIFICATION OF THE RELIGIOUS HYPOTHESIS

How the Verification of Religion Differs from the Verification of Science

The final test of the truth of any hypothesis is its relevancy to the matter it is supposed to explain as that is evidenced to us by judgments which carry immediate conviction. These judgments may rest upon sense perception in the familiar sense of that word or upon those more subtle insights we call intuitions. The difference between the certainty that comes to us as a result of untested intuition and that which comes to us through experiment is that in the latter case the judgment persists after all the available evidence has been considered, even though that evidence includes the introduction of new data which were not accessible when the first test was made.

In scientific experiments in the narrow sense we are continually devising new tests by which our hypotheses may be verified, and checking the results of our individual judgment by the concurrent observation of other competent observers. Similar criteria apply in the experiments of religion. They must be such as to confront the hypothesis to be tested with all available evidence which bears upon it and they must be confirmed by the independent testimony of other competent persons who have made the test for themselves.

But there is a difference in the religious man's use of experiment, which grows naturally out of the difference in the hypothesis to be tested. The hypotheses of science, as we have seen, deal with matters which admit of quantitative tests. The experiments of science, therefore, require the isolation of particular elements which lend themselves to measurement or enumeration.

But in religion we are dealing with life as a whole and no such dissection is possible. The subject of the experiment is man himself as he faces the mystery of life or its tragedy. The thesis he wishes to establish is that there is a good God who is adequate to his need, and the only way he can do this is to live as if God were what he assumes him to be and note the results that follow. This is what religious men have been doing ever since history began and this is what they are doing to-day.

The name which we give to this practical acceptance of the religious hypothesis is faith. Faith in the sense of the acceptance of a postulate not admitting of complete logical proof is to be sure not confined to religion. Science, too, as we have seen, lives by faith —faith in the validity of the basic assumptions without which scientific procedure in any form would be impossible. But the faith of religion differs from the faith of science as the conception of God, which is the

object of religion, differs from the conception of nature, which is the object of science. Faith, in the religious sense of that term, has an intimate and personal character which the faith of science lacks. To
have faith in God as the religious man understands
faith does not mean simply to believe that God exists.
It does not mean even to believe that God has the
qualities which answer to man's deepest needs. It
means to act in ways that are consistent with that belief. It means not simply to trust, but to prove one's
trust by obedience. The story of religion is the story
of men who have had faith in this sense and of the
transformations which have resulted in their lives and
in the life of society. It is a story of test by experiment.

The Religious Life as the Way of Validating Faith in God

The most familiar form of experimental test, and
in the last analysis the determining one, is the religious life itself. The difference between a religious
man and one who is irreligious is not that one is
necessarily better than the other but that one includes God among the realities of his universe, with
which he feels himself in some living practical relation, while the other does not. One test of the reality
of God then must obviously be that as individual men
gain in wisdom and experience, as they understand
better the conditions of knowledge and the dangers of
hasty and ill-considered judgments, as they enter un-
derstandingly into the new world which modern sci-

ence has opened for them and draw the appropriate consequences for practice, they still find it reasonable to believe in God.

This does not mean, of course, that they will continue to think of God just as their fathers did, or even that they will use the same words to describe what they believe themselves to have experienced of him, but that when we study their lives we shall still find them conscious of the presence of an ultimate reality, mysterious yet worshipful, to which they relate themselves in practical ways of worship and service.

How man's relation to God shall express itself in detail will differ in the case of differing individuals. The experiments of religion differ from those of science not simply in the fact that their subjects are men and women living their normal life in the world but also in the fact that as individuals each of them sustains a relation to God which is in some respects unique. No two of them, therefore, will express that relation in the same way. To one consecration will mean commitment to a life of intense activity. To another it may find expression through contemplation.[8] The uniformity of result, which is the ideal of scientific experiment, is ruled out from the start.

[8] Professor Santayana reminds us of the fact, too often overlooked, that contemplation as well as action makes powerful demands upon the emotional nature. "It is only a passionate soul that can be truly contemplative. The reward of the lover, which also chastens him, is to discover that in thinking he loved anything of this world he was profoundly mistaken. Everybody strives for possession; that is the animal instinct on which everything hangs; but possession leaves the true lover unsatisfied: his joy is in the character of the thing loved, in the essence it reveals, whether it be here or there, now or then, his or another's."—*The Realm of Essence* (New York, 1927), p. 16.

But this does not mean that no social tests are possible. Across the differences, whether of types or of individuals, common unities make themselves felt. In spite of the revolutionary changes which separate us from the men who wrote our Bible, we have not outgrown the Twenty-third Psalm or grown up to the Thirteenth Chapter of First Corinthians. Widely as they may differ in thought and in practice, those who have a vital experience of God recognize one another. Gandhi, Hindu though he be, feeds his spirit on the Christian Gospels, and many Christian missionaries, while understanding the reasons which lead Gandhi to disclaim the Christian name, recognize in him a soul by nature Christian.

But we do not adequately describe the extent of the social tests which may be used in verifying the religious hypothesis when we call attention to the fact that widely separated individuals may share a similar religious experience. There are religions—Christianity is a notable example—that think of God as revealing himself not simply in relationships to individuals, even though they be relationships of love, but in a radical transformation of society as a whole. Christians find ground for their faith in the existence and control of the Christlike God, not only in the changes which they see taking place in individual lives but in the fact that as they study the history of which these lives are part they see evidence of the operation of a principle of good-will, able to bring about a co-operation and sympathy between people and races not possible in any other way; and con-

versely, they find that when peoples refuse to follow
the dictates of this principle they are involved sooner
or later in consequences that are socially, as well as
individually, disastrous.

It is on this combination of the individual and the
social test that the full verification of the Christian
hypothesis must depend. Like every universal religion, Christianity must appeal to the future for its
complete justification.

To many persons this way of winning certainty of
God has seemed too difficult and complicated and they
have tried to find a short-cut to the verification desired by putting the whole weight of the proof upon
some single event, or group of events, which once established would not need to be retested. The argument for miracle in the conventional form is such a
short-cut. The effort here is to discover some event so
different in kind from those included in the system of
orderly happenings we call nature as to carry on its
face the evidence of being an immediate revelation of
God. But we have seen[9] that at two points the effort is
unsuccessful. For one thing it is never possible to
prove of any alleged miracle that it may not at some
later time be shown to fall within the system of nature. For another there is nothing in the mere occurrence of an event, however wonderful, that carries
with it any guarantee of divine revelation. It is the
quality of the event, its relation to what precedes and
to what follows, the insight it furnishes, the help it af-
fords, which alone can assure us of its divine meaning.

[9] Cf. pp. 79, 80.

But these are aspects which can be appreciated in their full significance only in the light of the later history, in other words as the hypothesis the alleged miracle is supposed to confirm is subjected to the test of repeated experiment. This is in fact the real ground on which miracles have been believed in by all who have made vital use of them in their religion. They have believed in them because there was something in the quality of the alleged miraculous events which seemed fitted to reveal God and they have continued to believe in them because the truths conveyed fitted into their structure of the universe as later experience has led them to conceive of it.

Worship and Service as Parallel Forms of the Test by Experiment

It is not then in special acts which can be isolated from their environment but in the course of life as a whole that the final test of the religious hypothesis is to be found. This test has two main aspects. One is worship; the other is service.

In worship we practise the presence of God. Forgetting for a moment the reasons which had led us to believe in God, forgetting equally the consequences which may follow from our faith, we concentrate our attention upon the qualities which make God adorable. Discovering in him power and wisdom, goodness and love, we give ourselves up to the joy of the discovery.

In service we turn back to the world to draw the practical consequences of our discovery. We ask ourselves what it means for our own lives and for the life of others that there exists such a God as we have found, and we act on what we see, trying as best we can to be strong, as he is strong; wise, as he is wise; patient, as he is patient; loving, as he is loving.

Separable in thought, these two aspects of the test are indissolubly connected in practice. "We love," says the writer of the First Epistle to John, "because he first loved us."[10] But he hastens to add, "He that loveth not his brother whom he hath seen, how can he love God whom he hath not seen?"[11]

In our own day we have laid so much emphasis on the second sentence of the Apostle that we have been tempted to forget the first. Partly in reaction from an other-worldly and impracticable religion, partly under the simple pressure of social need, with its crowding demands upon instant attention, we have emphasized the human side of our religion to the neglect of the divine and we are only just now beginning to discover the danger of our over-emphasis. No doubt the path of love to God may lead through love to man, but what if man as we see him to-day is unlovely? Then we need to correct our first unfavorable judgment by a more extended vision as we learn what the Apostle meant when he wrote, "We love because he first loved us."

What religion adds to ethics is just this consciousness of the divine presence by which all our human relationships are transfigured and glorified. From the imperfect and disheartening experiences of our daily

[10] I John 4: 19.   [11] 5: 20.

life we turn back to our closet that in communion with the Eternal we may regain our sense of balance and proportion and win poise and courage for the testing of the new day. But prayer, as Jesus has taught us to conceive it, will fulfil its true function only as we go out from our experience of worship to translate our love of God into answering love of man.

Christian Missions as a Way of Checking the Individual Test by Co-operative Experiment

The intimate relation between religious faith and ethical conduct may be illustrated in the missionary activity of the Christian church. That activity is designed to persuade those who do not now share the Christian faith in a God of love to accept that faith for themselves and to join those who now accept it in the attempt to make it universal. In other words, it is an effort to enlarge the scope of the test by experiment by extending it from selected individuals to society as a whole.

The attempt to win mankind as a whole to the acceptance of some particular form of religious faith is characteristic of the so-called missionary religions: Buddhism, Mohammedanism, and Christianity. Each professes to possess truth of universal validity and each attempts to justify this claim by practical activity. There have been religions that have made no claim to universality and there have been periods in the history of each of the great religions when missionary zeal has flagged. But such times have been looked back upon by later generations as periods of decadence. The great days of Christianity, as of Mohammedanism and of Buddhism, have been the days of their missionary triumphs.

From the point of view of the student of comparative religion the significance of the missionary enterprise, whether carried on by Christians or by the representatives of any of the other great religions which make claim to universality, is that it sharpens the issues which are at stake. It brings the representatives of the different faiths together under conditions which make it possible to determine what they have in common and wherein they differ, and so defines more clearly than would otherwise be possible the issues to be determined in the co-operative experiment in which they are all alike engaged.

These issues are the issues which have engaged our attention all through the present study—whether there be a God, and if so what he is like. The Christian missionary goes to men of other races and countries as witness to a God who deserves worship and requires service. In this he is only repeating to them what the representatives of their own religions have already said. But he goes on to add to his affirmation that God exists, a description of what God is like and what kind of worship and service he expects of men. The God in whom the Christian believes is himself love and requires love of his worshippers. The Christ, through whom he believes that God reveals himself, is not simply Savior of the individual but founder of the Kingdom of Love. To the Christian, therefore, there can be no permanent separation between indi-

vidual piety and social morals. God must evidence his
presence not only through personal helpfulness but
through social control.

Thus it appears that the issue to be determined
by the outcome of the missionary experiment is two-
fold; First, whether it is reasonable to believe in a
God who sets the ideal for man and with whom it is
possible for him to have practical relations of worship and service. Secondly, which of the different
possible ways of conceiving of God is most in accord
with the facts and which of the possible ways of worshipping and serving him is best adapted to realize
man's right relation to him. The first defines the
points on which all who hold any form of the religious
hypothesis differ from all those who reject it. The
second defines the point on which those who hold different forms of the religious hypothesis differ from
one another.

We may find a suggestive analogy in the attitude
of scientists toward the scientific hypotheses about
which they differ. Two contrasted interests motivate
them in the experiments on which they are engaged.
One of these interests is to show that, whichever of the
competing hypotheses gives the most adequate explanation of the phenomena which are under investigation, it is consistent with the major assumptions which all who engage in scientific experiment
share, namely, that nature presents an orderly system of relationships which lends itself to interpretation through the method of scientific experiment. The
other is to show that of the proposed alternative ex-

planations one rather than the others best conforms
to all the facts. The first defines the point on which all
who use the scientific method differ from those who
do not. The other defines the point at which those
who use this method differ from one another.

The Christian missionary, like the scientist, approaches his experiment with a double interest. He
desires in the first place to confirm the faith which is
common to all devout persons in a deity in some true
sense accessible to man, with whom he may have personal relations. He wishes in the second place to show
that of all the ways of conceiving God and of all the
ways of worshipping and serving him that which has
been revealed and illustrated by Jesus Christ is the
most reasonable and satisfying.

The latter attempt is now often regarded as pre-
sumptuous. So far as the Christian missionary movement adds its testimony to the witness of the other
great religions to the existence of a good God, it is
welcomed. But when Christians go beyond this and
claim for their own religion a superiority over Buddhism or Confucianism, the claim is resented as both
irrational and impertinent. If God wishes to reveal
himself, it is argued, why not let him reveal himself
to each people and to each age in his own way? What
is good for the Christian may not be good for the
Buddhist and *vice versa*. In science, to be sure, it is
recognized that there cannot be one standard for one
people and another for another. The laws of political
economy are as applicable in India or in China as in
Great Britain or in the United States. What is true

is true universally and what is economically sound in principle is sound everywhere. But religion apparently is an exception. Here, many of our contemporaries believe that individual preference must have right of way and that there may be as many religions as there are peoples.

It may be admitted that there is a way of presenting the Christian case against which these objections are in place. Where the attempt is made to impose upon every convert a standard which excludes the possibility of individual variation; still more, where the beliefs and practices natural to our Western civilization are forced upon people brought up in a very different environment without regard to the lessons they have already learned from their own religious teachers, the result cannot fail to be disastrous. Even within Christianity itself we have seen that it is impossible for one generation to transmit its beliefs to another unchanged. If God be the living God, ceaselessly active in nature and in history, we should expect that each generation will have something fresh to learn about him, and if each generation, why not each race or type of civilization? To commend Christianity to the Buddhist need not mean that Christians have nothing to learn from Buddhists, or that they do not recognize in Buddhism a revelation of the same God whom they worship.

But because we recognize large truth and value in the ethnic faiths it does not follow that there is no difference between them and Christianity or that Christianity has nothing to contribute to them which they lack. Just what the difference is and what the exact value of that contribution may be, it is the main object of the missionary experiment to determine. To assume with many of the critics of missions that there is no inherent difference between religions which makes it reasonable to expect that one rather than the others can make good its claim to be the universal religion is not only to prejudge the result of the experiment but, what is more serious, to make it impossible. For it is only the man who believes that he has found in his religion some truth of permanent and essential value who will have the patience and courage to make the sacrifice which is required for the effort to share it with others.

What is needed then is not the abandonment of the missionary experiment, but its continuance under conditions which make for its highest success. This requires on the part of those who engage in it not only sympathy with the good in other faiths and an open-mindedness which will make them quick to recognize and eager to accept the truths which have come to mankind through these faiths, but also such an intelligent understanding of the principles of their own religion as will make it possible for them to distinguish between its transient and its permanent features. There are some convictions common to all the greater religions which appear to be rooted in human nature itself and there seems to be no likelihood that man will ever outgrow them. There are other beliefs which the progress of knowledge is showing to be inadequate or false. There are permanent differences of type which recur in every civilization and in every religion. The real significance of the comparison between religions begins to appear when, after these eliminations have taken place, we contrast the elements that remain. It is through such comparison, carried on in the spirit of co-operation and sympathy, that our understanding of the real nature of religion will be most speedily advanced and our definition of the hypothesis which is in process of testing will be rendered most accurate and informing.

4. The Christian Way of Dealing with Evil

Two Ways of Dealing with Evil

We may illustrate the Christian way of vindicating faith in God in connection with the most serious of all the obstacles to faith, namely, the experience of evil. By its success in dealing with evil every religion must in the last analysis be judged.

There have been religions that have tried to dispose of evil by ignoring it. They have refused to recognize its presence and when the brute facts have been too patent to be overlooked they have explained them away. Christian Science is the latest of man's attempts to achieve universal well-being by denying that there is any such thing as evil. But the common-sense of mankind has refused to accept this easy solution.[12] Whether we look to the East or to the West,

[12] Mrs. Eddy herself, if her latest biograpber is to be trusted, while denying the existence of sickness and death, had much to say of malignant animal magnetism. And this magnetism, while in

to a mystical religion like Buddhism or to an ethical religion like Christianity, it is from man's experience of evil that we must take our departure. In his pain man turns to religion for healing, in his sin for forgiveness, in his futility and ineffectiveness for fulness of life. The great religions have been religions of redemption.

There have been two ways in which men have believed that redemption may come. One is through the removal of the causes which produce evil; the other through a change in the attitude of the persons to whom it comes. Scientists have concerned themselves primarily with the first of these ways; philosophers with the second. The scientist's way of dealing with evil is to discover its causes, that so far as they are removable he may eliminate them. The philosopher's way of dealing with evil is to fortify men against its demoralizing effects by explaining why evil is what it is and by pointing out the uses it is fitted to serve. Religious leaders welcome both these contributions and gladly make use of them. But their work begins where that of science and of philosophy stops. It is the office of religion to supplement man's resources for dealing with evil through the new energies which faith in God makes available either for its removal or for its conquest. Where evil can be prevented it becomes a religious duty to fight it. Where it is inevitable the religious man will accept it as permitted by God, and through its acceptance win peace

theory a purely mental thing, proved in fact to have many of the characteristics of the more familiar evils which afflict us common mortals.

and power. Both ways of dealing with evil may be illustrated in Christianity.

No religion has faced the facts of evil more frankly than Christianity. None, therefore, has more to teach about the service which religion can render us in our struggle against its ravages. Whether we consider its physical aspect, as pain, its moral aspect as tragedy or as sin, or its total effect in futility and ineffectiveness, we find it illustrated in the experience of the founder of Christianity. His mission led him to the Cross, symbol alike of pain, of sin, and of death. Yet it is in the Cross that Christians of every age have found the ground of their brightest hope. For in the Cross they have seen God dealing with evil and overcoming it.

Christians have often isolated the Cross from its surroundings, as though it expressed the experience of salvation in its totality. On the Cross, they have taught, Jesus made atonement for the sins of the world and in the acceptance of his divine sacrifice man finds freedom and peace. But crucial as is the Cross for our understanding of Jesus' work and central as has been its place in the religious experience of his followers, it expresses only one aspect of Jesus' attitude toward evil. He came not only to repair the consequences of evil but to remove its causes. This was true of pain. He healed the sick and comforted the sorrowful. It was true of sin. He preached repentance and set an example of brotherly love. It was true most of all of failure. He came that man might have life and might have it abundantly.[13] So long as

13 John 10:10.

evil was preventable he fought it. Only when it became inevitable did he accept it as God's will.

This attitude has been characteristic of his followers ever since. No religion has taken the battle against evil more seriously than Christianity. There is no form of evil which Christians have not fought with all the resources that the knowledge of the time has made available. Where there was sickness they have established hospitals. Where there was ignorance they have founded schools. Where there was injustice they have been among the first to protest. We think of Father Damien and his mission to the lepers of Molokai. We think of Florence Nightingale and her service in the hospitals of the Crimea. We think of David Livingstone as he matched his unaided skill against the open sore of the world. There is not a country to which Christian missionaries have not gone with their ministry of service, not a people or race which has not experienced the uplifting and reconciling influence of Christian love.

But when love has done its utmost and failed, what then? Then the other way of dealing with evil is called into play. What cannot be evaded must be accepted as God's will and, through acceptance, may be transformed into moral power.

Jesus as an Example of the Christian Way of Dealing with Evil

Jesus is our example here, as in all else religious. In the Garden he faced the apparent failure of his life work. We hear his prayer, "Not my will but thine be done." And we note the consequences that followed. Through acceptance of suffering as God's will we see him master his despair and win courage for the agony which awaits him. As we watch, we begin to understand how religious faith can transform apparently insuperable evil into creative power.

What the Master experienced in Gethsemane has been repeated in the experience of multitudes of his disciples. Explain it as we may, there is something in religious faith which can put a meaning into the inexplicable and find a joy in the intolerable. We remember the brave words with which Latimer cheered the aged Ridley when he faced the mounting flames: "Be of good cheer, Master Ridley, for we shall this day light such a candle in England as shall never be put out." Joan of Arc, burned as a heretic by the church which after four centuries canonized her as a saint, finds her way into the hearts of men to whom religion, but for her faith, would be only a name. And it seems only yesterday that another woman, older in years but as young in spirit, left as her legacy to the generation who would read her story the words: "Patriotism alone is not enough."

We used to smile at the naïveté of the old alchemists who thought that they might find a way to transmute dross into gold. Our most recent synthetic chemistry has shown that their aim was not impossible. Religion too has its alchemy. Through faith in God it can transmute evil into an instrument of good. St. Paul could say, as he looked back over years full of suffering, physical and mental, that he had found

in his adversities matter for rejoicing. And when we
contemplate experiences such as his our sense of the
dignity of human nature is profoundly strengthened
and our belief in its spiritual possibilities is infinitely
enhanced.

"Along the earth and up the sky
   The Fowler spreads his net:
O soul, what pinions wild and shy
   Are on thy shoulders set?
What wings of longing undeterred
Are native to thee, spirit bird?

What sky is thine behind the sky,
For refuge and for ecstasy?
Of all thy heavens of clear delight
Why is each heaven twain,
O soul, that when the lure is cast
Before thy heedless flight,
And thou art snared and taken fast
Within one sky of light,
Behold the net is empty, the cast is vain.
And from thy circling in the other sky the lyric laughters
   rain."[14]

Religion has its explanation of the mystery. It is
the spirit of God which comes to life within the spirit
of man, the spirit that can never die since it is itself
the spirit of life immortal.

How Prayer Helps Us to Master Evil

If we ask religious people how these divine resources are to be made available, they will tell us that
it is through prayer. It was on prayer that Jesus re-

[14] Moody, Wm. Vaughn, *Poems and Poetic Dramas* (New York,
1912), pp. 195–196.

lied to carry him through each recurrent crisis. It was through prayer that he was able to meet the crowning agonies of Gethsemane and of the Cross.

And when we realize what prayer is we can understand why this should be. Prayer is the name that we give to the practice of the presence of God. It is the way we make explicit to consciousness the relation in which we stand to God all the time and so release for practical purposes those resources of wisdom, of inspiration, and of renewal which are always available for us, but which, for lack of intelligent direction, we allow to go largely unused.

Prayer that is sincere and effective can do many things for us; but the greatest thing that it does is to lift us to a new level of experience. It enlarges the sphere of our appreciations. We see things in a new perspective. We feel things with a new intensity. Through contact with God, the supreme excellence, we gain courage to resist temptation, strength to endure suffering, motive to oppose wickedness, love to forgive those who misunderstand and persecute us. It is through prayer and what prayer means that we come to grips with the most formidable of all the obstacles to certainty, the fact of evil in our own lives and in the life of the world.

Prayer helps us to deal successfully with the challenge of evil, partly by enlarging the resources we can bring to bear upon the struggle against evil, whether in ourselves or in others; partly by reminding us that we are not alone in our struggle. God, who is himself love, is a sharer in our experience and by the transformation wrought in ourselves through the fellowship of his love we are encouraged to believe that in the end love will be everywhere victorious.

This hope of final victory robs present defeat of its sting. To his enemies, the earthly life of Jesus might seem to end at Calvary. In the experience of his disciples, Calvary became a stage in a continuing and triumphant life.

So prayer stimulates present resistance to evil by reinforcing hope in its ultimate defeat. In every age we find men and women who through its practice have been able to deal successfully with evils which they themselves believe, apart from that aid, would have proved too strong for them. It has helped them to bear pain, the wearying pain of the body and the even more agonizing pain of the mind, not by immediate removal of its causes but by introducing into consciousness new factors which have increased man's power to endure, and often to master pain altogether. It has helped them to deal with moral failure, restoring their self-respect, even while it sharpened their moral insight. Above all, it has given them a new purpose in life, helping them to see that no failure is final but that in a very literal sense defeat and agony—not the agony of the body only but the agony of the spirit—may prove a door leading into a larger life.

If it be said that prayer does this, not by any magic power drawn from outside of man but by revealing to him the law of his own nature and enabling him to live accordingly, and that it is possible for people who follow these laws to reach similar results even apart from faith in God, we shall not be concerned to deny it. The God we worship is the God of the whole world and the laws science studies are ways of his working. The point is that for multitudes of people prayer, however understood and explained, does the things that we have called attention to and that they are things that we greatly need to have done. Through faith in God men have been able to discover a beneficent meaning in experiences which to others spell only unreason and despair, and from this discovery have gained renewal, courage, and inward peace. Why then should we not believe that a similar experience may be possible for those men and women to whom it has not yet come?

How Prayer Bears Fruit in Love

Yet important as is the contribution which prayer must make to the test by experiment, it cannot be isolated from the other form of the test, the life of loving service. As religion adds to ethics the dynamic that comes from the realization of the presence of God, so ethics adds to religion the assurance that the God so discovered is the Lord of all life, and not simply of a part. In ethics we apply the ideal we have appropriated in prayer to the concrete conditions in which our life is lived and so justify our confidence that that ideal has universal significance.

There is rich material at this point to be gained from the study of history. Among the most powerful influences in the development and application of ethical ideals has been the leadership of great religious personalities. From Jesus' day to our own, love to God has borne fruit in love to man.

We are only now beginning to discover what forms human love should take in our complicated modern world. In the simpler world in which the New Testament was written the task of love was correspondingly simple. It took the form that Jesus has described in the twenty-fifth chapter of Matthew—visiting the sick, feeding the hungry, giving drink to the thirsty, clothing the naked, visiting the prisoners—the form we now know as charity. But to-day we see that such ministry as this, necessary and beautiful as it is, is dealing with the symptoms of the disease and not with its cause. Science has revealed to us, among other things, how sickness and poverty come about and has put into our hands powers which, if rightly used, will make it possible to make an end of them. So Christian love receives a new objective. It aims not only to make better and happier men and women, but conditions in which it shall be natural for them to be well and happy.

In our effort to assimilate the new knowledge which the social sciences are bringing us it is easy to exaggerate the novelty of their aim. Men often speak of the social gospel as if it were a new thing. But from the first, as we have seen, Christianity has been a social religion, setting no limit to the obligation of love. What science has brought us is not a new objective but a new technique. It has helped us to see more clearly than we did before the conditions which must be met if love is to come fully into its own.

The Social Gospel as the Rethinking of the Religious Ideal of Love in the Light of Modern Science

For one thing science shows us how much more complicated are the relations between individuals than we had supposed; how many factors go into making man what he is; factors temperamental, educational, political, as the case may be. It shows us that people are powerless to change much for which we blame them, at least at the moment. It helps us to realize, as we could not otherwise have done, the importance of the time element in human betterment; the need of patience; of sympathy; above all, of resourcefulness.

But science does not stop here. It goes on to point out to us the remedy for the evils it diagnoses. If it shows us what part environment plays in the moulding of character for good or evil, it shows us also how environment can be changed. Many evils like disease and poverty, which men had always supposed to be inevitable, we now know to be due in part at least to causes which we can control, and we are working together from many centers to control them. The story of the last three generations is a story of heartening progress, both in the discovery of the causes of human maladjustment and suffering and of their removal.

Some of our contemporary humanists draw the conclusion that what we need in our struggle against evil is not more religion in the conventional form but a more thoroughgoing use of those homely remedies which science puts in our hands, remedies physical, economic, or intellectual, as the case may be. For if society is to be redeemed it is men who must do the redeeming by becoming in all their relationships to one another what men at their best may be.

But the question still recurs. How is the needed change to be brought about? Science may show us what we ought to do and how we ought to do it. But who is to make us *want* to do it? Here religion meets our need with the contagion of personality, first human, and then divine. It was the love of Christians for one another, which, in a cruel and selfish age, won converts for the new faith. It is the practical demonstration of the fruits of love which to this day makes most persuasive appeal.

The Practicability of the Christian Ideal for Society

The assumption that the Christian ideal for society can be realized without the help of religion is less damaging than the assumption often made to-day that it can never be realized at all. There are many who tell us that over wide areas of life the Christian experiment has manifestly failed; that it runs counter to deep-seated instincts of human nature; that it asks of man the impossible, often the undesirable; that man is by nature a fighting animal and that he will continue to fight, if not in one way then in another; that all talk of a co-operative society, of a warless world, is a poet's dream.

In answer it may be said that to accept the principle that because man has fought in the past he will always continue to do so would make not peace only but all education impossible. For the fundamental thesis of modern education is that human nature can be changed. Many things which man has formerly done he has now ceased to do. Other things he has learned to do which he has previously never done. Dogmatism as to the future is out of place. We must await the test by experiment.

But we are not shut up to this inconclusive reply. Definite reasons can be given to account for the fact that we have made such slow progress in the application of the social gospel. As human history is measured, it is only yesterday that we acquired the knowledge which makes it possible for us intelligently to apply the principle of love to the conditions of our existing social life. In order to help our fellowmen successfully we must have knowledge as well as goodwill. We must not only wish our neighbor well; we must know what is really for his good. But even today this knowledge is in the possession of a small number of specialists and there are many questions of the greatest practical moment on which they are still uninformed. There is need of much research and experiment and an even greater need of education as to the results of past experiments before we can translate our ideals into accomplishments on an extended scale.

The essential thing is that we should accept the ideal, and at this point genuine progress has been made. Both in the church and without it the conception of human society as the scene of warfare among competing individuals is being vigorously attacked and the Christian ideal of brotherhood is accepted in wide circles as a standard not for the life of individuals only but for society as a whole.

The change that has taken place in the attitude of the churches toward social questions has been the subject of frequent comment. Along many different lines we see them enlarging their activities, interesting themselves in various questions of economic and educational reform, reconsidering their responsibility to the diverse issues of class and of race, and throwing themselves heartily into the new movement for the abolition of war.[17] All that this may mean in detail we are not yet in a position to say. For this we must wait for the time when the full implications of the

[17] This broader view of the church's social responsibility has been voiced in this country in the Social Creed of the Churches, a statement originally adopted by the Methodist Episcopal Conference in 1908, and subsequently reaffirmed by the Federal Council. (*The Social Work in the Churches*, ed. F. Ernest Johnson (New York, 1930), p. 123.) In Great Britain it was responsible for the series of documents issued by Copec, a conference called at Birmingham in 1925 to consider the Christian's duty in the field of politics, education, and citizenship. In the international sphere it found impressive illustration in the Conference on Life and Work, which was held in Stockholm in 1925, and which summed up its view of the church's social responsibility in the following impressive sentences:

"The Conference has deepened and purified our devotion to the Captain of our Salvation. Responding to His call 'Follow Me,' we have in the presence of the Cross accepted the urgent duty of applying His Gospel in all realms of human life—industrial, social, political and international."—(*The Stockholm Conference on Life and Work*, 1925, ed. by G. K. A. Bell (London, 1926), p. 711.)

A convenient compendium of information on the social attitudes of the churches of the United States is given in *The Social Work of the Churches*.

positions taken shall have been understood and the appropriate consequences for conduct shall have been drawn.

What is going on in the church is symptomatic of a change which is taking place in society at large. From many different centres and in many different forms the crusade for a unified and a brotherly society is being carried on. The ideal of a League of Nations in which all civilized peoples shall be represented and in which they shall co-operate one with another in fighting common enemies like war and disease, is winning recognition in circles which hitherto have been little suspected of idealism. One would not ordinarily go to a committee of international bankers for a homily on the brotherhood of man. Yet in their recent report to the home governments the Young Committee on Reparations used the following significant words:

"The solution of the reparation problem is not only a German task but in the common interest of all the countries concerned; and it requires the co-operation of all parties. If their attitude should be tinged with antagonism, even with suspicion or a desire to create or continue one-sided economic discriminations, a settlement perfectly feasible with good-will would sooner or later encounter difficulties, so that the long, slow, patient task of reconstruction in Europe would be definitely retarded. For without good faith and mutual confidence all agreements, all guarantees, are unavailing.

If, on the other hand, our proposals are adopted with good-will by all concerned and the rest of the world has confidence in the constructive value of this mutual accord, then, indeed, there can be no reasonable doubt that the agreement will be capable of complete fulfilment and the nations con-

cerned will be brought to a higher level of economic stability and of mutual understanding than ever before."[18]

Nor are these fine words a matter of pious hopes
alone. In many different spheres of human interest
definite progress is being made toward translating
aspiration into achievement. If the Kellogg Pact is
to be regarded as an expression of hope rather than
as a register of accomplishment, the League of Nations, in Europe at least, is a fact, and with every
year is making itself a more assured place in the plans
of statesmen and in the confidence of peoples. And
with the war against war on the large scale goes also
a ceaseless war against all those petty wars which
within each nation breed suspicion, envy, and fear.
In the relations between races; in the strife between
capital and labor; in our attitude toward the weaker
and more dependent members of society, our children,
the aged, the sick, the unemployed, we are developing
a social conscience and situations which would have
been accepted a generation ago as a matter of course
are felt as an intolerable scandal. In his book, *Christianizing the Social Order*,[19] Walter Rauschenbusch
wrote some impressive chapters in the story of this
sensitizing of the social conscience, and were he still
living he would find new chapters to be written. The
mediæval ideal of a society which should be in fact as
well as in name Christian is being recovered to-day.
Christendom has been rediscovered.

It is at this point that the issue raised by con-

[18] New York *Times*, June 9, 1929.
[19] New York, 1912.

temporary humanism must meet its final test. Is it true that human love alone supplies adequate motive for social reform? Or is there added power to be derived from the Christian's faith in the good God who shares his life with the life of others and who, when our human power fails, can reinforce our weakness with his unfailing strength? Faith in the God of love has inspired the life of love in the past and for many inspires it to-day. To people carrying burdens too heavy for their unaided strength it has brought the assurance of a divine helper and the reinforcement of an unconquerable hope. Is there any reason to doubt that it will continue to do so in the future?

This conception of God as a fellow-worker with man in the making of a new world puts the social gospel in its true setting. The social gospel is simply our way of defining what love must be and do if it is to reach men and women in the complicated world that modern science has remade for us. It is the latest rethinking of the test by experiment.

CHAPTER VII

THE CERTAINTY OF TO-DAY AND THE HOPE FOR TO-MORROW

1. How to Win Assurance of God for Oneself.

   The Final Issue: Discovery or Revelation—Where God Is Speaking to Us To-day—How to Make God's Presence Real.

2. How the Hope of Immortality Enlarges the Range of Possible Verification.

   Immortality as Opening Possibilities of Future Experiment—Ways of Justifying the Hope of a Continued Life After Death.

3. How to Deal with the Uncertainties That Remain.

   The Remaining Margin of Uncertainty—How to Deal with the Uncertainties That Are Due to the Limitations of Our Knowledge—How to Deal with the Uncertainties That Are Due to the Instability of Our Environment.

It is through what we do even more than through what we think that our certainty of God must be won. Thought may help to remove the obstacles which make faith difficult, but in the last analysis it is the will that must speak the deciding word. God is speaking to us in many ways: through the beauty of nature, through our intuitions of the right, through the teachings of history, through the discipline of suffering, through the appeal of human need. But his words will pass unheeded unless we listen to them and they will remain ineffective unless we act on them. In religion, as on other sides of our life, we win assured conviction only by living out our faith to the utmost and finding that it will stand the test. Our experience of God as a present factor in our lives, inspiring us to fight evil while it is still preventable and transforming it into his messenger when it is inevitable, is the ground of our confidence that he will continue to reveal himself to us during our life here and that when this life is over he will provide opportunity for further fellowship in a life to come. From this vantage ground of assured conviction we may contemplate with a quiet mind the uncertainties that still remain, confident that God, who has given us enough light for to-day, will supply the necessary guidance for to-morrow.

1. How to Win Assurance of God for Oneself

The Final Issue: Discovery or Revelation

To sum up. There are two kinds of certainty: the certainty which is the aim of the exact sciences and the certainty which is attainable in common life. The first is reached by eliminating all factors which involve judgments of personal taste or appreciation and confining the inquiry to those aspects of reality which admit of accurate measurement and on which, therefore, complete agreement of all unprejudiced observers is possible. The second deals with matters into which personal value judgments necessarily enter and on which, therefore, complete agreement is not at any one time to be expected. To the scientist, whether he be a physicist, a chemist, a biologist, or a psychologist, a man is a machine whose mechanism is to be analyzed and the mode of whose operation is to be investigated. To the ordinary person he is a comrade to be trusted, a leader to be followed, an enemy to be feared, or a friend to be loved. Yet in the second realm, as in the first, it is possible to reach a high degree of practical certainty. And we risk our lives on judgments that take this certainty for granted.

Our certainty of God is of the second kind. It is a certainty that invites to experiment and is confirmed by its results.

It is through action then rather than through thought alone that religious certainty is finally to be won. That is the conclusion to which the whole course of our study has been leading us. The enterprise in which we are engaged is not a classroom debate. It is a laboratory experiment. Reflective thought may analyze the possibilities and marshal the arguments on one side or the other, but of itself it can never carry us beyond probability. Only the will can translate probability into certainty and make the God of whom others have told us real to us.

But is such willing within our power? If what we have been learning about certainty is to be trusted, are we not shut up to the conclusion that certainty is the one thing that cannot be willed? Either it comes to us or it does not. When it comes we have it. When it is absent it is because the conditions which produce it are lacking. Pragmatic philosophers may write eloquently about the will to believe, but belief is the one thing that is not in the power of the will. Whether conviction is won depends in the last analysis upon the character of the evidence that is presented and the appeal that that evidence makes to the contemplating mind.

And if God were only an idea of the mind, this would be all that could be said on the matter. But if God is what religion assumes that he is—a living reality, with which we are in first-hand contact through all sides of our nature—the situation is different. Here action is necessary in order to create, or at least to appropriate, the evidences with which thought can deal. One of the most fruitful sources of skepticism, now as in every preceding age, is the fact that men have been content to treat God as an object of belief. They have not gone on to test him as a reality to be experienced.

We have an analogy in our personal relationships. Nothing that any one can tell us about another person can be a substitute for that confident assurance that comes to us through the first-hand contact of life. We learn to know other persons by living with them, doing things together, sharing the give and take of personal intercourse.

This is the way the great masters of religion tell us they have won their assurance of God. They have learned to know him by living with him, doing things in which he shared, experiencing the give and take of personal intercourse.

For the relationship between God and man, we must never forget, is a reciprocal relationship. It is not man who takes the initiative in seeking after God: but God who goes out to find man. Religious faith is not simply discovery, though it is that. It is response. The God of living religion is the self-revealing God.

God's revelation comes to different people in different ways, but however it comes it is always a surprise. Something has happened to make life different —something unanticipated, something creative. Where once there was darkness, now there is light. Where once there was strain, now there is inner harmony and peace. How the change happens we may never completely understand. We know only that it has taken place and that it has altered the experience of living for us.

The varying forms in which the assurance has come have led many to question the interpretation which religious people have put upon it. What has seemed to one person or to one age a revelation from God has often failed to win unquestioning response from its successors. As we follow man's experience of God through the centuries we seem to be studying a chapter of man's own life history in which the varying interests of succeeding generations have been projected upon the larger canvas of the universe. It is indeed this spectacle of change which furnishes the humanist with one of his strongest arguments. Why not confess frankly, that God is the reflection of human desire, and be content to remain within the limitations which are set for us by our human nature?

Yet man has never been willing to do this. There is something in him that refuses to be satisfied with the limitations of his own finiteness. As he contemplates nature he is haunted by the persistent sense that what he can see and feel and touch is not the whole. There is an unseen reality which is reaching out to him, a world of undiscovered meanings to which he seeks the clue. Religion is born of that haunting sense of otherness. In the words of one of the great mystics, the soul, when it contemplates nature, "beholds all things as the work of God's hands." They are "messengers that tell us that there is a something still more, I know not what, that remains unspoken, a something still to be uttered, a profound impression, a deep knowledge of God."[1] To ask man to give up faith in this other that is *more* than man is to ask him to become *less* than man.

Often, no doubt, man's effort to reach this reality has failed. Often, when it has seemed to succeed it has led to results which taken at their face value are conflicting. There is nothing in this that ought to discourage or surprise us. Religion is not the only side of man's life in which certainty has been won slowly through the age-long testing of apparently contradictory beliefs. The story of science, too, is the story of many conflicting opinions, each generation claiming certainty for conclusions which later experience has shown to be untenable. Indeed, one of the great temptations of historic religion has been to accept too trustfully the certainty which contemporary science has offered.

But just as the remedy for the mistakes of science is more science, so the correction of the misconceptions of religion must come from more religion. As the story of science is the story of the gradual emergence and progressive verification of certain dominant convictions concerning the nature of the universe and our way of understanding it that persist in spite of change, so the history of religion is the story of the emergence and progressive verification of certain permanent convictions concerning God and man's way of knowing him.

To learn what God means for the religious man, we must leave the classroom of the theologian and the

[1] St. John of the Cross, *Canticle,* stanza vii, p. 44.

library of the philosopher and study those persistent convictions which recur from age to age in the lives of people to whom religion is a vital experience. We do not regard the conclusions of scientists as invalidated because people who have never given attention to science tell us they cannot understand them. Why then should we regard the convictions of religious people as invalidated because they are not shared by multitudes who have never taken the trouble to test them?

This reminder will help us to appreciate the true place of the will in our search of certainty. We cannot will ourselves into the knowledge of God. Our certainty must come to us as it has come to all who have won it before us, by means of an inner constraint that brooks no denial. It must come as love comes, or joy, or peace, because the conditions of its coming are present. But this does not mean that we can do nothing to prepare the way for its coming or to keep it vivid when it comes. There are at least two things that we can do. We can direct our attention in the place where God is speaking and, when the message has come, we can act upon it.

Where God Is Speaking to Us To-day

In religion, as everywhere else in life, attention is the key to success. Yet we are often too busy or too preoccupied to give the time and the concentration that is needed. Meditation in the sense in which it has been practised by the great masters of religion has become all but a lost art. For this there is but one remedy. We must change our habits. We may not be able to will God's presence, but we can desire the things that his presence would bring and we can take time to wait for them and to prepare our spirits for their reception.

This cannot be done quickly, or without effort and practice. We must take the time that is needed and we must plan our days so that this time can be had; ample time, so that we shall not be hurried; fresh time, when we are not tired. We must treat our search for God at least as seriously as we treat our friendships or our business.

Let us suppose that this initial step has been taken. We have learned through our contact with others what a living faith in God may mean for human life and we are ready to do whatever may be necessary to win a similar faith for ourselves. But here a new difficulty confronts us, the fact that God has no definite physical embodiment by which we can localize his presence as we localize the presence of the human persons with whom we have intercourse. Where in this familiar world in which we are living day by day can we find our point of contact with God?

This is a difficulty which is felt with peculiar force by a generation like our own which is preoccupied with things. Yet on closer inspection it may prove that the real reason why we find it hard to recognize God is not that we have no definite means of physical contact with him but that we have so many. It is not that God is not speaking but that he is speaking on every hand.

God is speaking to us through natural objects; in the order which we find in the universe; in the beauty which is common to flower and to star; in the ceaseless succession of living creatures; in the marvel of our own bodies; in the uses which nature serves in our own lives.

God is speaking to us in our own souls; in those intuitions of the good, the true, and the beautiful that arise within us we know not how and furnish us with the standards by which we judge the choices and the conditions of life as better or worse, beautiful or ugly, useful or harmful.

God is speaking to us in human history, in the persistent social ideals through which our understanding of his character gains definiteness and his purpose is made explicit; in the succession of great personalities who have been most vividly aware of his presence; through the books that record their insights and perpetuate their memory; and through the institutions that carry on the work which they have begun.

God is speaking to us in the suffering that harrows the soil of the soul, the suffering that disciplines our own lives, the suffering in other lives that stirs our sympathy.

God is speaking to us, above all, through human need; the need that we feel in ourselves of inspiration, of guidance, and of renewal; the need of others who turn to us for help that we are often impotent to give. It is his voice that comes to us across the ages in that familiar word of Jesus, "Inasmuch as ye have done it unto one of the least of these my brethren, ye have done it unto me."[2]

But often we fail to apprehend the meaning of these familiar voices and among the many things that they are saying we overlook the thing that matters most.

It is here that the experience of others can help us. Authority, as we have seen, cannot serve as a substitute for our own first-hand knowledge, but it can suggest to us where we should look for knowledge and remind us of some of the things we may expect to find. Among the many objects that compete for our attention, it can point us to those that have been most helpful to others—to the Bible, for example, or to the sacrament, or to Jesus himself. These, it tells us, are sources for the knowledge of God that we cannot afford to neglect. We cannot tell what they will have to say to us till we have made the necessary contact. But we can at least try the experiment. We can direct our attention to the places where men before us have found God.

How to Make God's Presence Real

And when we have looked and seen, what then? Then we must act on what we have seen.

How can we tell that it is really God with whom we have to do and not simply some subjective creation of our own imagining which we have made for ourselves by wishful thinking? Partly by comparing our own conclusions with those of others who have made

[2] Matt. 25:40.

their experiment with God before us, but chiefly by *acting* on the insights which have come to us and by finding that the results follow which we should expect.

This is the way in which all assurance of reality must finally come. In order to know, we must act. The test Jesus gave his disciples for distinguishing between opinion and reality is still a valid test to-day: "If any man will do his will he shall know of the doctrine, whether it be of God or whether I speak of myself."[3]

The test is valid on all sides of our experiment with God. It is valid in the realm of the mind. We turn to God because he gives us the answers to our ultimate questions. But we can only tell whether the answers are to be trusted by treating the world as if it were the kind of a world in which God is the basic fact. If God is really what our faith assumes, there is nothing in what science can tell us of which we need to be afraid. We must keep our minds open, therefore, to the new knowledge which is coming to us through the researches of our contemporaries and be ready at any time to make the needed readjustments in our thinking. If God in whom we put our trust is really God, no redefinition can rob us of our experience of his reality. But redefinition can help us to distinguish things that are essential from things that are transient and so intensify our sense of the real presence of God.

Jesus' test is valid in the realm of the emotions. God, as we have seen, is the supreme object of wor-

[3] John 7: 17.

ship, opening to us the possibility of a fellowship which gives joy to living and inspiration to service. Let us act as becomes those who hold this faith. Let us cultivate the habit of thankfulness, looking upon each experience that comes to us as God's gift and learning from it the lessons which it was meant to teach.

And let us do this all along the line, not simply with the bright side of life, but with the dark side, the sorrows that life brings to us, its disappointments, its failures. Let us treat these as our great predecessors in the religious life have treated them, as opportunities for new insight and sources of new power. Let us see in failure an aid to detachment, in suffering a summons to fortitude, in sorrow a school of sympathy.

Above all, Jesus' test is valid in the realm of conduct. God, as we have seen, sets the standard for our actions. He reveals himself as love and as requiring love in us. Let us do the thing love demands, directly in the narrow circle where we have control over our action, indirectly in the wider circle which we can influence through the formation of public opinion. Whether there be much that we can do or little, let us do what we can with all our might.

It is not necessary for the application of this test that our thought of God should be definite at all points. It is necessary only that we should act out our insight so far as it has come. If God be the truth, we shall find him most surely by holding to what seems to us true. If God be the good, we shall meet him most certainly by doing what seems to us right.

This means in the first place that we must live by our *appreciations*. In whatever form goodness and beauty reveal themselves to us we must recognize them as revelations of God and follow where they lead. Wherever we find people loving the beautiful and striving after the good we must recognize them as our brothers and co-operate with them as far as they will let us. Intellectual difficulties we must face honestly, with the frankness they deserve, but where, as will more often prove the case, the difficulty is moral—in the temptation to self-indulgence or the unwillingness to face the consequences of our own insight—we must be ruthless with ourselves. At the root of much loose thinking is moral laxity. Only the disciplined character can expect to see things as they are.

In the course of this process of self-discipline we shall expect to find our idea of God changing. Some things we thought essential will fall into the background; others of which we had made little will take the central place. Things that we took for granted will seem wonderful. Old words will fill up with new meaning. We shall appreciate, as we could not have appreciated at first, what it means to believe that the God of all the world is a God of love.

As our ideas of God are enlarged and transformed, our estimate of other people will alter accordingly. The conventional catalog of sins will mean less and less to us as we realize more and more how persuasive and elusive a thing is selfishness. At the root of every specific breach of human relations we shall find a divided self living for the gratification of the impulses of the moment because it has not yet discovered the larger self which is formed for God. Wherever we find men who have the larger vision, seeing the whole of which we are a part and living by what they see, we shall recognize comrades in our upward struggle, disciples and followers of the Christ, even if they do not yet know him by name, members of that living church which is some day to win the world for God. We shall be reinforced in our struggle to do the right by the knowledge that our victory will be helpful to them.

These comrades in faith are to be found not only within the Christian church. The church, as we see it to-day, is divided into two parts, separable, yet indissolubly connected: the outward church of form and ceremony, custom and tradition, and the inward spiritual church of faith and hope and love. These two are in a state of constant strain as those who see the new vision strive to lift their fellows to their own point of vantage and win for the church as a whole the enrichment that comes with enlarging experience. And what is true of the church is true of mankind. Here, too, there are comrades struggling toward the same goal and facing the same obstacles. Some we recognize across the barriers of unfamiliar creed and rite, but more are unknown to us even by name. These have their contribution to make to the great experiment and only through the co-operation of us all can it be carried at last to success.

2. How the Hope of Immortality Enlarges the Range of Possible Verification

Immortality as Opening Possibilities of Future Experiment

There is solid ground then for our faith in a progressive self-revelation of God in history, a revelation which is to find its consummation in a society which realizes in fact the ideal which the prophets and sages of mankind have anticipated in imagination, a society of free men co-operating for common purposes under conditions which respect the individuality of each.

Yet when all has been said that can be said the gap between accomplishment and ideal remains appallingly great. What revolutionary changes must needs take place in the most Christian of so-called Christian nations before the gap between ideal and reality is even measurably bridged. It is hard enough to make one Christian, harder still to make a Christian church. To make a Christian nation is a task to stagger the imagination; to make a Christian world may well seem all but impossible. Yet this, no less, is the goal which our religion sets us. Is it possible to believe that a consummation so far-reaching can take place within the limits of our human lives?

For a few brief years indeed Christians believed it possible. In the first joy of rediscovering the risen Jesus, his disciples expected that he would speedily return to earth to establish the kingdom whose coming he had preached; and there are groups to-day for

whom the expectation of an imminent personal coming is still a living faith. But as generation has succeeded generation, and century century, the early
expectation has faded, and most Christians have
either abandoned it altogether or postponed it to an
indefinite future.[1]

Confronted by this dilemma religious thought has
in the past reached out beyond the span of the present earthly life and has transferred to the limitless
reaches of eternity its faith in the complete fulfilment of hopes denied here.

In our own days the vision of an immortal life has
grown dim for many and multitudes have learned to
look to science or to art or to simple human brotherhood for the uplifting and unifying influences once
provided by the communion of the living with the
dead. But there are others, and among them some
eminent men of science, who are recovering the lost
hope in unexpected ways.

Whether the expectation of a continuing life will
be justified in fact, only the future can determine.
That is the last and greatest issue to be submitted to
the test by experiment. In that test we shall all have
a part, for to all of us, sooner or later, death is coming and as we answer its summons we shall prove each
for himself whether death ends all or whether it ush-

---

[1] We have an interesting secular parallel in the attitude of the two
schools of socialists toward the social revolution. The Communists
confidently expect the coming of world revolution in their own life-
time; whereas the great body of Socialists, like the great body of
Christians, postpone the coming of the new society to an indefinite
future.

ers us into a new stage of the great experiment of which our life here is the beginning.

Ways of Justifying the Hope of a Continued Life After Death[4]

In the meantime it may be of interest to remind ourselves of the reasons which are leading many modern thinkers to believe that this wider extension of the test by experiment will be open to us.

Some of them have come to their belief by the methods of science. They believe that there are data already accessible to us which prove the continuance after death of individual self-consciousness with its distinguishing attributes of intelligence, affection, will, memory, and the power of communicating with others. Many of our contemporaries, and among them some persons of eminent scientific attainment— whether an increasing number it is not easy to tell— believe themselves to have received such communications and find support for a religious interpretation of life here from the fact that they have done so. They see in the communications which are coming to them to-day the continuance of phenomena similar to those recorded in the Gospels and so a confirmation of the faith of the early disciples that they had had personal communication with the risen Jesus. To them, as to the great body of Catholic Christians, living and dead together form one unbroken society with continuing affections and interests.

[4] For a fuller statement of the reasons for faith in immortality *cf.* Brown, W. Adams, *The Christian Hope* (New York, 1912); *The Creative Experience* (New York, 1923).

Others, unconvinced by the scientific evidence adduced, base their belief in immortality on philosophical arguments of a more general character. Unless we accept the hypothesis of man's continued existence after death, they tell us, life seems to involve us in a fundamental inconsistency. We see nature through countless æons working toward the production of beings with consciousness and character. We see these beings disciplined by struggle and responsibility into families, churches, and states. We find them more and more forced by the stern school of experience to recognize their kinship with one another and to devise forms of organization in church and state which will make it possible for them to act together for common ends. And then, just at the time when they are ready to profit by the lessons they have learned, or, what is still more strange, when the process of learning has scarcely begun, we see them abruptly caught away from the scene of their training with their tasks half done and their lessons half learned. If we are to believe in purpose at all, such an outcome seems a mark either of irony or of futility. But if this life be not all, if what we see here be only a training for other work in other realms, then all that is here incomplete falls into place as part of a larger continuing process.

If it be objected that we cannot tell what life after death will be like, that we cannot conceive of the continuance of consciousness when the present physical organs of consciousness have been destroyed, the answer is that no new stage of existence can be anticipated until it occurs and that in view of the amazing revelation of the new possibilities of physical communication brought to us in the last few decades the word "impossible" should be ruled out of court. Not proven—we may well admit that. We are dealing with a hypothesis of faith. The point is that it is a reasonable hypothesis and that if entertained it would bring order into a part of our thinking where there is now chaos.

Is this all that can be said? I think not. There is still a third way of approach to the problems of immortality more easily accessible to most of us. It is the way of practice. We may live with those we love as if they were alive and we may find to our surprise that for us they are.

Humanist writers have often proposed as substitutes for the theist's belief in the continuance of self-consciousness after death that we should solace ourselves with the immortality of memory and the immortality of influence. It is true, they tell us, that there is a sense in which our dead are still alive. They live for us in memory, as we direct our attention to what they once did and were and find it still as vivid to our consciousness as though they were really here. They live for us in a deeper and more vital sense in the influence they have had upon us and still have, an influence that is operative in all that we say or do.

All this is true, and it is good that it is true. It is one of the glories of personality and one of its mysteries that in these very real senses, even if in no other, it survives death. And it is one of the tragedies of our short-sighted view that we do not use this fact as we might to enrich and sweeten life. As there is a practice of the presence of God through prayer and consecration, so there may be a practice of the presence of our beloved dead through memory and loyalty. With them, as with the living, communion in a very real sense may be possible.

What are we to conclude from these facts? That our dead are really dead and that it is only our imagination that makes them seem alive? Why not rather that they are really living and that it is because they are alive that memory and influence continue?

Let no one try to rob us of this faith by pointing us to the psychological processes that explain the memory and influence that are in question. Those same processes are functioning and in similar ways, in our relations with people who, everybody admits, are still alive. The question we need to answer is not how we come to have this consciousness of continuing life—let the psychologist deal with that as he will—but what conclusions we are to draw from the fact that we do have it. The point I would make here is that it is at least a legitimate hypothesis that the influence which those who have died exert upon us here is but part of a wider influence which may be operating upon others in ways unknown to us and which may ultimately operate upon us when we enter upon the new conditions into which the life after death is to introduce us.

We may find an analogy in our attitude toward

faith in God. We cannot demonstrate God's existence. We can only give grounds for believing that
faith in him is reasonable and appeal to the future
for confirmation. But in the meantime we may take
that faith as our working hypothesis and find it confirmed by its ability to unify the life we are living
here. So we cannot demonstrate faith in personal immortality. We can only give grounds for believing
that faith in immortality is a reasonable faith and
appeal to the future for confirmation. But in the
meantime we may take that faith as working hypothesis and find it reinforced by its ability to ennoble and
glorify the life we are living here.

3. How to Deal with the Uncertainties That Remain

The Remaining Margin of Uncertainty

In such ways as these we may hope to diminish the
area of uncertainty and to win an assured basis of
conviction upon which we may safely build our lives.
But when all has been done that can be done, there
will still remain an irreducible margin of uncertainty
that so far as we can see cannot be affected by anything that we can do. What ought to be our attitude
toward this uncertainty?

First of all, we should be clear that the fact of
continuing uncertainty ought not to surprise or to
dismay us. Certainty and uncertainty, as we have
seen, are not inconsistent. In a growing world we

find them side by side, and must expect to find them there.

But that does not mean that there is nothing that we can do about our uncertainties. On the contrary, there are certain quite definite things that we can do. As we have a responsibility for the certainty that is open to us, to make it as sure and as stable as we can, so we have a responsibility for the uncertainty that we cannot avoid, to use it so that it will be helpful and not disturbing.

There are two forms in which this responsibility meets us. It meets us in connection with the uncertainties which are due to the limitations of our knowledge. It meets us also in connection with the uncertainties which are due to the instability of our environment.

In each case our duty is plain. As those who trust God, we must accept the uncertainties which still surround us as his will for the discipline of our character and for the deepening of our life.

How to Deal with the Uncertainties That Are Due to the Limitations of Our Knowledge

In the realm of the mind it is not hard to do this. It is a great thing to have a God whom we can know. It would be a pitiful thing to have a God of whom we knew all that there is to be known. Just because God is God, our thought of him must always be incomplete, our certainty the compass by which we steer our way across a shoreless sea.

Just after dawn one summer day I stood on the hill

that rises above Lake Chautauqua and watched the sun struggling to make its way through the clouds. The lake was covered with a sea of golden mist. One was conscious of light and glow and warmth and motion. But as the mists rose and fell, circled and returned, and curved themselves into fanciful and graceful shapes that were never twice the same, the sun still remained hidden. One knew that it was there. One could see its glow; one could feel its warmth; one rejoiced in the beauty of its handiwork. But the sun itself remained unseen.

So it is with the revelation of God. We say: If only I could see him as he is! But there are good reasons why this direct vision is not granted us. One reason that is often given is that if we should see God as he really is we could not bear the sight, even as our eyes cannot bear the sight of the sun. God is so great that unless he should restrain his power it would destroy us. He is so pure that if we should see ourselves as he sees us we should be overwhelmed by the thought of our own sinfulness. His love is so amazing that even when Jesus tells us of it it seems too good to be true.

But even if this were not true and we could bear to see God as he is, there is another reason why it may be well that our knowledge should be incomplete. If we could see completely the side of God which he is turning to us at the moment, we might be content with our partial view and look no further. So, to lure us on to a fuller understanding of his purpose, God keeps something of himself always in reserve. We have enough light for to-day. But what is coming to-morrow is hidden from us. That the new dawn will bring to those who wake to greet it.

How to Deal with the Uncertainties That Are Due to the Instability of Our Environment

But there are other uncertainties with which it is not so easy to deal, the uncertainties that result from the instability of our environment. Fast as science may progress, it cannot overtake the dangers against which it is supposed to insure us. To-day, as nineteen centuries ago, in the midst of life we are in death. Each new invention brings its corresponding peril, each added power its fresh possibility of misuse. One may be as rich as Crœsus and as wise as Plato. No door has yet been found strong enough to bar a home against the entrance of calamity. Still the old prayer, "From battle, murder, and sudden death, good Lord, deliver us," voices a need that is real to multitudes of our contemporaries. In a world so unstable, where shall security be found?

There is only one way. It is the way that Jesus took. We must accept the fact of uncertainty, even in its most baffling and devastating forms, as God's will for our growth. We must think of it as God's call to courage, as his school of sympathy, as his danger-signal against self-indulgence, as his invitation to fellowship.

Hard as it is to do this, it would not present an insuperable difficulty if the uncertainty concerned ourselves alone. But when others are affected a new factor is introduced which accentuates the difficulty. In a world where love sets the standard there can be no solution of life's problems which concerns the individual alone. The outcome of each man's experiment with God becomes inextricably interwoven with the outcome of the experiment of all the others.

The wider setting of individual faith has in all ages presented a problem of peculiar difficulty to the sincerely religious man. The contrast between the world as it should be and the cruelty and suffering of the world that now is, has been the greatest stumbling block to sensitive and unselfish spirits. It was this contrast that Jesus faced as he went to Calvary. It is this which still throws the darkest shadows across the path of his disciples. Can anything be said to lighten this shadow and to relieve this strain?

This, at least, can be said, that in a moral world there must be shadows. Instinct may suffice as a guide for creatures without reason or conscience; but for men with characters to form there must be risks to face and burdens to bear. The quality in Christianity which has given it the strongest appeal to virile characters is that, in essence, it is a form of heroism.

But if for you and for me as individuals risks and burdens are necessary, must we not believe that they are also necessary for others. We who have struggled and suffered would gladly pass on to those we love the wisdom which our own trials and failures have taught us. But it cannot be done. God deals with the members of each new generation as if it were

the first. Life's inevitable experiences meet them in
their youth and vigor with the freshness of a surprise. Through uncertainty, through strain, through
suffering they are guided into an assured touch with
reality, and win at last, if faith and courage hold
firm, to the peace that passeth understanding.

We end as we began with Jesus' promise: "If any
man will do—he shall know." It is through action
that assurance must be won. The certainty which religion offers us is a practical certainty, the certainty
that comes to a man who follows the best he knows.
The religious life is adventure in heroism, an adventure which must justify itself by its results. We validate our belief in God by the life which such belief
makes possible in ourselves and in our fellowmen.

So, accepting our responsibility for to-day with
cheerful courage we contribute our part to that enlarging store of wisdom which will make assurance
easier for those who come after us. Living by the
light of a reasoned and tested faith, trusting the insights which come to us in our best moments, drawing
faith and comfort from the convictions of those who
have gone before us, we win for ourselves the certainty we need and we help to communicate it to
others.

BIBLIOGRAPHY

The brief list that follows makes no claim to exhaustiveness. From the vast amount of available material only those books have been chosen which seem to bear helpfully upon the subject of our present study. Those most likely to be useful to the general reader have been marked with an asterisk (*). Roman Catholic works are indicated by the letters R.C. in parenthesis.

BIBLIOGRAPHY

I. THE LOSS OF CERTAINTY IN CONTEMPORARY RELIGION

Ames, Edward Scribner: "Religion." New York, 1929.

Barnes, Harry Elmer: "The Twilight of Christianity." New York, 1929.

Burtt, Edwin A.: "Religion in an Age of Science." New York, 1929.

* Dewey, John: "The Quest for Certainty." (Gifford Lectures for 1929.) New York, 1929.

Foerster, Norman: "Humanism and America." New York, 1930.

* Horton, Walter M.: "Theism and the Modern Mood." New York, 1930.

Huxley, Julian: "Religion Without Revelation." New York, 1927.

Krutch, Joseph W.: "The Modern Temper." New York, 1929.

Leuba, James H.: A Psychological Study of Religion." New York, 1912.

* Lippmann, Walter: "A Preface to Morals." New York, 1929.

Otto, Max Carl: "Things and Ideals." New York, 1924.

Randall, J. H., and J. H., Jr.: "Religion and the Modern World." New York, 1929.

Randall, John H., Jr.: "The Making of the Modern Mind." New York, 1929.

"Humanist Sermons." Editor, Reese, C. W. Chicago, 1927.

Sellars, Roy W.: "Religion Coming of Age." New York, 1927.

"Whither Mankind." Editor, Beard, Charles A. New York, 1928, p. 313 f.

279

II. Ways of Reaching Certainty

Baillie, John: "The Interpretation of Religion." New York, 1928.

Bergson, H.: "An Introduction to Metaphysics." New York, 1912.

Burtt, E. A.: "Principles and Problems of Right Thinking." New York, 1928.

* Dewey, John: "How We Think." London, 1909.

* James, William: "The Varieties of Religious Experience." (Gifford Lectures for 1901, 1902.) London, 1902.

* James, William: "The Will to Believe." New York, 1897.

* Lyman, Eugene W.: "Theology and Human Problems." Boston, 1910.

* Lyman, Eugene W.: "Mysticism, Reason and Social Idealism." *Journal of Religion,* April, 1928.

* Montague, W. P.: "The Ways of Knowing." New York, 1925.

Morgan, W.: "The Nature and Right of Religion." Edinburgh and New York, 1927.

Murphy, Gardner: "An Historical Introduction to Modern Psychology." New York, 1929.

"The Psychologies of 1930." Editor, Murchison, Carl. Worcester, 1930.

Wallas, Graham: "The Art of Thought." London, 1926.

III. The Way of Authority

Adam, Karl: "The Spirit of Catholicism." Translator, McCann, D. J. New York, 1929. (R.C.)

Barth, Karl: "The Word of God and the Word of Man." Translator, Horton, D. 1928.

Brown, W. Adams: "Imperialistic Religion and the Religion of Democracy." New York, 1923.

Brunner, H. Emil: "The Theology of Crisis." New York, 1929.

Dodd, C. H.: "The Authority of the Bible." New York, 1929.

Fullerton, Kemper: "Prophecy and Authority. A Study in the History of the Doctrine and Interpretation of Scripture." New York, 1919.

Machen, J. G.: "Christianity and Liberalism." New York, 1923.

Martindale, C. C.: "The Faith of the Roman Church." London, 1927. (R.C.)

Martineau, James: "The Seat of Authority in Religion." London, 1890.

* Oman, John: "Vision and Authority." New York, 1929.

* Rawlinson, A. E. J.: "Authority and Freedom." (The Bishop Paddock Lectures for 1923.) London, 1924.

Sabatier, Auguste: "Religions of Authority and the Religion of the Spirit." Translator, Houghton, L. S. New York, 1904.

Stewart H. L.: "A Century of Anglo-Catholicism." New York, 1929.

IV. THE WAY OF INTUITION

* Baillie, John: "The Roots of Religion in the Human Soul." New York, 1926.

Bennett, Charles A.: "A Philosophical Study of Mysticism." New Haven, 1923.

* Brightman, E. S.: "Religious Values." New York, 1925.

* James, William: "The Varieties of Religious Experience." New York, 1902.

Laird, John: "The Idea of Value." Cambridge, 1929.

* Lyman, Eugene W.: "Mysticism, Reason and Social Idealism." *Journal of Religion,* April, 1928.

* Lyman, Eugene W.: "The Place of Intuition in Religious Experience and Its Validity as Knowledge." *Journal of Religion,* Vol. IV, 1924, pp. 113–132.

Otto, Rudolf: "The Idea of the Holy." Translator, Harvey, John W. London, 1923.

Perry, Ralph Barton: "General Theory of Value." New York, 1926.

Poincaré, Henri: "Science and Method." Translator, Maitland, Francis. New York, 1915.

Royce, Josiah: "Sources of Religious Insight." New York, 1912.

Sorley, W. R.: "Moral Values and the Idea of God." (Gifford Lectures for 1914, 1915.) Cambridge, 1918.

St. John of the Cross: "The Ascent of Mt. Carmel." Translator, David Lewis. London, 1922.

* von Hügel, Baron Friedrich: "Selected Letters 1896–1924." Editor, Holland, B. London, 1927. (R.C.)

* von Hügel, Baron Friedrich: "Essays and Addresses." Series 1, London, 1921. Series 2, London, 1926. (R.C.)

V. The Way of Reasoning

Burtt, E. A.: "Principles and Problems of Right Thinking." New York, 1928.

Eddington, A. S.: "The Nature of the Physical World." (Gifford Lectures, 1927.) New York, 1929.

James, William: "The Will to Believe." New York, 1897.

James, William: "Pragmatism." New York, 1907.

Jeans, Sir James: "The Universe Around Us." New York, 1929.

Morgan, C. Lloyd: "Emergent Evolution." (Gifford Lectures for 1922.) New York, 1923.

Morgan, C. Lloyd: "Life, Mind, and Spirit." (Gifford Lectures for 1923.) New York, 1925.

Macmurray, John: "Objectivity in Religion." In Streeter, B. H., et al, "Adventure." New York, 1928.

Millikan, R.: "Evolution in Science and Religion." New York, 1927.

Pupin, M. I.: "The New Reformation." New York, 1927.

"Science, Religion, and Reality." Editor, Needham, J. New York, 1925.

Sorley, W. R.: "Moral Values and the Idea of God." (Gifford Lectures for 1914, 1915.) Cambridge, 1918.

* Streeter, B. H.: "Reality." New York, 1926.

Thomson, J. Arthur: "Science and Religion." (Morse Lectures for 1924.) New York, 1929.

Webb, C. C. J.: "God and Personality." (Gifford Lectures for 1918, 1919.) New York, 1918.

Whitehead, Alfred North: "Science and the Modern World." New York, 1925.

* Whitehead, Alfred North: "The Function of Reason." Princeton, 1929.

VI. THE WAY OF EXPERIMENT

* Brown, W. Adams: "The Life of Prayer in a World of Science." New York, 1927.

* Heiler, F.: "The Spirit of Worship." Translated by Montgomery. London, 1926.

* James, William: "The Varieties of Religious Experience." New York, 1902.

James, William: "The Will to Believe." New York, 1897.

Jones, E. Stanley: "The Christ of the Indian Road." New York, 1925.

Jones, E. Stanley: "The Christ of the Round Table." New York, 1929.

* Knox, Geo. W.: "The Direct and Fundamental Proofs of the Christian Religion." New York, 1903.

Niebuhr, Reinhold: "Does Civilization Need Religion?" New York, 1928.

Rauschenbusch, W.: "Christianizing the Social Order." New York, 1912.

* Sperry, Willard L.: "Reality in Worship." New York, 1925.

* Streeter, B. H.: "Reality." (Chaps. 6 and 8.) New York, 1926.

"The Christian Life and Message in Relation to Non-Christian Systems." (Documents for the Jerusalem Conference, prepared by the International Missionary Council.) New York, 1927.

"The Church and Industrial Reconstruction." (By the Committee on the War and the Religious Outlook.) New York, 1921.

"The Social Work of the Churches. A Handbook of Information." Editor, Johnson F. Ernest. New York, 1930.

Ward, H. F.: "The New Social Order." New York, 1927.
* Wieman, H. N.: "The Wrestle of Religion with Truth."
New York, 1927.

VII. THE CERTAINTY OF TO-DAY AND THE HOPE FOR
TO-MORROW

* Brown, W. Adams: "Beliefs That Matter." New York,
1929.
Brown, W. Adams: "The Christian Hope." New York,
1912.
Brown, W. Adams: "The Creative Experience." New
York, 1923.
* Van Dusen, Henry Pitney: "In Quest of Life's Mean-
ing." New York, 1926.
Hocking, W.: "The Meaning of God in Human Experi-
ence." New Haven, 1922.
* Horton, W.: "Theism and the Modern Mood." New
York, 1930.
* Nixon, Justin W.: "An Emerging Christian Faith."
New York, 1930.
Roberts, Richard: "The Christian God." (Merrick Lec-
tures for 1929.) New York, 1929.
Ross, J. Elliott: "Truths to Live By." New York, 1929.
(R.C.)
* "Ventures in Belief: Christian Convictions for a Day of
Uncertainty." Editor, Van Dusen, Henry P. New
York, 1930.
"Whither Christianity?" Editor, Hough, Lynn Harold.
New York, 1929.

INDEX

INDEX

Adaptation, 156; evidences of in the inner world, 162.

Ambrose, 122.

Ames, E. S., 16.

Anglo-Catholics, 110.

Anthropomorphism, 173; two kinds of, 177.

Apostles' Creed, 104.

Appreciation, contribution of to certainty, 262.

Arguments for the being of God, 155–160; permanent significance of, 160–162; why no longer convincing to many, 164.

Aristophanes, 32.

Aristotle, 26.

Arnobius, 135.

Art, mystical element in, 142.

Assurance, 253, 254.

Astronomy, 26.

Atonement, 234.

Augustine, St., 45, 85, 102, 122, 170.

Authority, 6, 36, 66, 72, 74, 78, 80, 108, 259; artist's use of, 74; as a form of revelation, 86; broader conception of, 89; contribution of to our appreciation of God, 107–108; emotional appeal of, 111, 113; external, why necessary, 84; function of in society, 112; in religion, 99; in what sense Jesus is, 111, 114; limitations of Roman Catholic, 92; modern revolt against, 94–95; of Bible superseded by authority of churches, 94; our responsibility for use of, 90; place of in science, 13; place of in religion, 13; relation to intuition, 148; universality of the method of, 85; uses of, 116; use of by religious people, 100; use of by science, 97–98;

what is meant by, 83; what it can do for us, 97; what it contributes to our thought of God, 101–103; when necessary, 87.

Babbitt, Irving, 15.

Baillie, John, 211.

Balfour, Arthur, 121.

Baptism, 110, 226–227, 233.

Barth, Karl, 135.

Beauty as revelation, 147.

Bebel, 19.

Belief, emotional factor in, 53–54; forms in which it meets us, 87; four ways of testing, 65–67; how its nature determines the method of its testing, 71; natural history of, 61; non-rational factors in, 48; physical basis of, 50; possible attitudes toward inherited, 87; quality of, 57; reasons which make retesting necessary, 64; what it means to validate, 62.

Bell, G. K. A., 105, 245.

Bennett, Charles A., 129.

Bible, 77, 79, 85, 89, 91, 93, 100, 131, 133, 147, 217, 259; as authority, 93; as source of Christian belief, 103; contrast between Protestant theory and practice, 100; Luther's use of, 93, 94.

Birmingham, 245.

Brightman. E. S., 164.

Brooks, Phillips, 45, 170.

Brown, William Adams, 30, 266.

Brunner, H. Emil, 135.

Bryan, William J., 54.

Buddhism, 214.

Burtt, E. A., 201, 210.

Bushnell, Horace, 123, 203.

Butler, Bishop, 157, 165.